HISTORY

PAPER 2 CAUSES AND EFFECTS OF 20TH-CENTURY WARS: THE FIRST WORLD WAR

JOE GAUCI

OSC

OSC

OSC IB Study & Revision Guides
Published by OSC Publishing,
Belsyre Court, 57 Woodstock Road,
Oxford OX2 6HJ, UK

T : +44 (0) 1865 512802
F : +44 (0) 1865 512335
E : osc@osc-ib.com
W: osc-ib.com

IB History SL & HL Paper 2 Causes and Effects of 20th-century Wars: The First World War
9781910689349

9349.01
© 2018 Joe Gauci

The material in this Study & Revision Guide has been developed independently of the International Baccalaureate Organisation. OSC IB Study & Revision Guides are available in most major IB subject areas. Full details of all our current titles, prices and sample pages as well as future releases are available on our website.

Cover and Chapter Openings Image: Scene on the Somme Front
Source: Ernest Brooks (photographer), the National Library of Scotland (CC BY 4.0). http://digital.nls.uk/first-world-war-official-photographs/archive/745465968 (accessed 12 April 2018)

Printed and bound by CPI Group (UK) Ltd, Croydon CR0 4YY
www.cpibooks.co.uk

PREFACE

The First World War is a topic that I became interested in about 20 years ago when I started teaching it to my students at Malvern and organised a series of annual study visits to the battlefields and war cemeteries of France and Belgium. Standing at the Menin Gate in Ypres when the last post was sounded or at the towering Thiepval Monument, which commemorates the 72,000 soldiers who were killed on the Somme but have no known grave, were profoundly moving experiences that have stayed with me ever since.

I have taught IB Diploma History at Malvern College since 1992, as well as on OSC Easter and Summer Revision Courses for the past twenty years. I have always enjoyed writing history essays and helping students prepare for essay-based examination papers. For a history student, generally essay writing is the biggest challenge they will face. Writing a very good or excellent essay requires both a very secure understanding of a lot of historical information but also mastery of a range of essay-writing skills: interpreting the question; planning an effective approach to the question and creating a clear structure; writing an introduction that identifies the themes or factors the essay will explore and the thesis of the essay; developing a clear line of argument and keeping focused on the title; selecting and deploying precisely an appropriate range of supporting evidence; and, finally, restating the main argument of the essay in order to provide a strong conclusion.

Joe Gauci

CONTENTS

LIST OF FEATURES

HOW TO USE THIS GUIDE

This guide contains detailed notes on the causes, practises, and effects of the First World War. At the end of the guide, you will find sample essay questions, with a student's answer, accompanied by suggestions for improvement in one case and my own answer to a second question, followed by space for you to include your own points. By examining these questions, you will be able to test your understanding and recall of that material and, in addition, practise your essay-writing skills.

What parts of the IB History syllabus is this guide useful for?

1. Primarily, this guide is intended to help SL and HL candidates who are studying the the First World War as a case study for World History Topic 11: Causes and Effects of 20th-century Wars for Paper 2.

2. In addition, it will be of help to HL candidates who are studying Paper 3: Syllabus Section 13: Europe and the First World War (1871–1918), as part of HL Option 4: History of Europe.

Feature boxes

This guide includes a range of feature boxes that highlight essential information and help you navigate through the book. You will find the following types of colour-coded box in the main text and in the margins:

CROSS-REFERENCE	Where else to look in the guide for more information on a topic.
KEY INFORMATION	Key facts, issues, viewpoints, and terminology. Key terms appear in bold when they are first mentioned in the main text and a definition is provided at the bottom of the page. All key term definitions are collated in the glossary at the end of the book.
TIMELINE	Helps you to visualise and contextualise important events.
KEY PERSPECTIVES	An overview of the differing historical perspectives on important events in the First World War. To access the higher marks on Paper 2 and Paper 3, examiners expect candidates to show an awareness of and evaluate differing historical perspectives.

PAPER 2 EXAM INFORMATION

What do you need to know about Paper 2?

- The examination lasts *one and a half hours*.
- It is divided into 12 sections, each on a different world history topic.
- Causes and Effects of 20th-century Wars is Topic 11.
- Two essay questions will be set on each topic, so there are 24 questions in total.
- Candidates have to answer two questions, each chosen from *different* topics.
- The maximum mark for each question is 15.
- For HL candidates, Paper 2 is worth 25% of the total assessment.
- For SL candidates, Paper 2 is worth 45% of the assessment.
- Topic 11 covers various types of war, for example: total (e.g. the World Wars); limited (e.g. the Falkands War); civil (e.g. Spanish Civil War); and guerrilla (e.g. the Greek Civil War).
- All questions will be open-ended, and candidates can use any relevant case study or case studies (where two examples are asked for).
- The IB syllabus specifies that the following aspects of Topic 11 should be studied:
  - Causes of war
  - Practices of war and their impact on the outcome
  - Effects of war.
- Some questions will demand discussion of wars from more than one region (there are four world regions as defined in the IBO handbook).

ESSAY-WRITING ADVICE

- You must spend a few minutes carefully looking at the paper and weighing up the choice of questions, before you make up your mind on which two questions to answer.

- Look very closely at the wording of the questions, making sure that you understand their implications and what you need to address in your answer.

- Pay particular attention to 'command' words such as: 'to what extent', 'examine', and 'compare and contrast'. In the case of 'to what extent was any 20th century war you have studied a total war?' you must weigh up the ways in which it was and the ways in which it was not total, reaching a conclusion about whether it was entirely, largely, partly, or not at all, total. 'Compare and contrast the causes of two twentieth century wars' would require you to examine the similarities and the differences between their causes. 'Examine' means analyse or scrutinise, so 'examine the results of one twentieth century war' would require you to identify the key effects of the war politically (both in domestic and international terms), economically, socially and technologically, evaluating which were most important.

- Always plan your answer, spending at least two or three minutes doing this for each essay, if not longer (but no more than five to six).

- Give equal time to each essay you write. Do not be tempted to spend much longer on one at the expense of the other.

- Answer the question. Keep your approach analytical, do not drift in to a description of events. Focus tightly on the question; do not deviate.

- Perhaps the best way of ensuring that each paragraph is linked to the title, is to check that your first sentence (the 'key' sentence) is making a statement that directly answers the question.

- For each point that you make, provide an explanation of what light that point sheds on the question/why it is significant and also present evidence or a precise example to support it. So, the drill should be: *Statement, Explanation, Example.*

- Always write in complete sentences and be as clear as you can in your use of English. The clearer your English, the more effectively you will communicate your points to the examiner.

- Always write a proper introduction. This must identify the key issues raised by the question. You should also outline your thesis, the line of argument that your answer will take.

- Make sure that you leave time for a proper conclusion. The main purpose of this is to restate your key arguments.

- Do not feel that you have to pack your answer with references to differing schools of historical interpretation and named historians. You will get credit for such historiographical references, where used appropriately, but do not insert them just for the sake of displaying your knowledge if they do not contribute to answering the question.

- Whatever information you insert in to your answer, whether in the form of a fact, a statistic or a quotation, do make sure that you explain its significance and how it answers the question. If you do that, your essay should remain focused.

KEY FIGURES IN THE FIRST WORLD WAR

THEOBALD VON BETHMANN-HOLLWEG (1856–1921) Career Prussian bureaucrat who was chancellor of Germany from 1909 to 1917. He was effectively forced out of office in 1917 as a result of pressure from Germany's two most senior military commanders, Hindenburg and Ludendorff.

OTTO VON BISMARCK (1815–98) Prussian politician who unified Germany in 1871 and then, as chancellor of Germany, created a system of defensive alliances to keep Germany secure. He resigned in 1890 partly because his foreign policy outlook differed from that of Kaiser Wilhelm II.

ALEKSEI BRUSILOV (1853–1926) Career Russian military officer who commanded Russia's Eighth Army from 1914 to 1916 before being promoted to commander-in-chief of the South-Western Front in March 1916. Brusilov launched a massive offensive against Austro-Hungarian forces in May 1916, which initially was very successful but ultimately ground to a halt. He was briefly commander-in chief under the Provisional Government between May to August 1917. He later returned to military service from 1920 to 1921 in helping the Bolshevik government fight against Poland.

WINSTON CHURCHILL (1874–1965) British politician who was in charge of the navy from 1911 to 1916 as first lord of the admiralty. He strongly advocated the Gallipoli Campaign in 1915, which proved a costly failure. He became minister of munitions in 1917 in Lloyd-George's government. He was later Britain's prime minister (1940–45) during the Second World War.

GEORGES CLEMENCEAU (1841–1929) Leader of the Radical Republican Party in France, and prime minister from 1906 to 1909 and, again, from 1917 to 1920. Known for taking an aggressive stance towards Germany, including at the Paris Peace conference in 1919, he was nicknamed 'the Tiger'.

GABRIELE D'ANNUNZIO (1863–1938) Leading Italian writer and nationalist politician. Already a famous author and poet before the First World War, he served in the Italian Air Force in the war. From 1919 to 1920, he and a group of nationalist supporters illegally occupied the port of Fiume, which he was forced to withdraw from in 1920.

FRIEDRICH EBERT (1871–1925) Moderate German socialist politician who became chancellor of Germany following Kaiser Wilhelm II's abdication in November 1918. Ebert's government signed the armistice with the Allies on 11 November 1918. Ebert was elected president of Germany in 1919 and died in office in 1925.

ERICH VON FALKENHAYN (1861–1922) Chief of the German general staff from September 1914 to August 1916, he was replaced after the failure of his attempt to bring France to the point of collapse by attacking Verdun.

FRANZ FERDINAND (1863–1914) Nephew of Franz Josef, emperor of Austria-Hungary, and, from 1896, heir to the Austro-Hungarian Empire. He was assassinated in June 1914 in Sarajevo by Gavrilo Princip, a Bosnian Serb nationalist.

FERDINAND FOCH (1851–1929) French general who was appointed Allied commander-in-chief in May 1918 and oversaw the Allied armies' successful offensives in the last months of the war.

DAVID LLOYD GEORGE (1863–1945) British Liberal politician, chancellor of the exchequer (1908–15), minister of munitions (1915–16), minister of war (1916) and prime minister (1916–22). At the Paris Peace Conference, he pursued a more moderate policy towards Germany than Clemenceau of France but tougher than that of President Wilson of the USA.

SIR EDWARD GREY (1862–1933) Liberal politician and British foreign secretary from 1905–16.

SIR DOUGLAS HAIG (1861–1928) Career soldier who was appointed British commander-in-chief at the end of 1915, replacing Sir John French, and remained in that post until 1921. A controversial figure whom many blame for the failure of the Somme and Passchendaele offensives, but who has been defended by some historians more recently.

PAUL VON HINDENBURG (1847–1934) Career soldier who commanded German forces fighting the Russians in 1914. He was promoted to German commander-in-chief in 1916, a position he retained until 1919. He was later elected as president of Germany in 1925 and re-elected in 1932. He appointed Hitler as chancellor in 1933.

MUSTAFA KEMAL (1881–1938) Career officer in the Ottoman Empire who came to national and international attention in leading Turkish defences against the Allies at Gallipoli in 1915. He led Turkish resistance to the terms of the Treaty of Sèvres, which involved a successful war with Greece in 1920–22, and became president of the Turkish Republic following the abdication of the last Ottoman emperor in 1922.

ALEXANDER KERENSKY (1881–1970) Moderate socialist politician who was appointed to Russia's Provisional Government in March 1917 as minister of justice. Kerensky served as minister of war from May to July 1917, launching the unsuccessful 'Kerensky Offensive' in June 1917. Kerensky was Russia's prime minister from July to November 1917. Kerensky's government was overthrown by Lenin in November 1917 and Kerensky went into exile in France.

JOHN MAYNARD KEYNES (1883–1946) Economics lecturer at Cambridge University at the start of the First World War, joining the Treasury in 1915. He was an economic adviser to Lloyd George as part of the British delegation at the Paris Peace Conference in 1919. Keynes resigned from the delegation in protest at the harsh economic terms drawn up for Germany and published a stinging criticism of the terms of the Versailles Treaty in 'The Economic Consequences of the Peace' (December 1919).

VLADIMIR ILICH ULYANOV BETTER KNOWN BY HIS REVOLUTIONARY ALIAS LENIN (1870–1924) Russian Marxist revolutionary from the 1890s who became leader of Russian Bolsheviks. In exile for most of the period 1900–1917, he returned to Russia in April 1917, a month after the February Revolution ended the Romanov monarchy. Lenin denounced Russia's participation in the First World War and successfully overthrew Russia's Provisional Government in November 1917. He took Russia out of the First World War in March 1918 and then led the Russian Communist Party to victory in the Russian Civil War in 1918–21. He died in 1924.

ERICH VON LUDENDORFF (1865–1937) German career soldier who served as Hindenburg's chief of staff in 1914 and masterminded the German victories at Tannenberg and the Masurian Lakes. From 1916 to 1918, he and Hindenburg had overall control of Germany's armed forces, with Ludendorff viewed as the more dynamic of the two. In 1918 he organised a massive German offensive in the west which broke through the Allied lines but ultimately stalled. He resigned in October 1918. He later took part in Hitler's Beerhall Putsch in Munich in 1923.

HELMUTH VON MOLTKE (1848–1916) Chief of the German general staff from 1906 to 1914. Wilhelm II had him replaced in September 1914 after the failure to achieve a quick victory against France.

BENITO MUSSOLINI (1883–1945) Appointed editor of the Italian Socialist Party's newspaper, *Avanti*, in 1912, he was sacked because he supported Italy's intervention in the First World War. During the war, Mussolini set up a nationalist newspaper, *Il Popolo D'Italia*, and also joined the Italian Army. In 1919 Mussolini created the Fascist movement, initially a mix of left- and right-wing views. In 1921 Mussolini relaunched his movement as the Fascist Party and moved it firmly to the right politically. In 1922, after threatening to march on Rome with his armed supporters, King Victor Emmanuel appointed Mussolini as prime minister. From the beginning of 1925, Mussolini transformed his regime into a dictatorship.

TSAR NICHOLAS II (1868–1918) Son of Alexander III of Russia, he ruled Russia from 1894 until the February Revolution of 1917. He then abdicated and was executed by the Bolsheviks along with the rest of his family in 1918.

VITTORIO ORLANDO (1860–1952) Liberal politician, first elected to the Italian Chamber (Parliament) in 1897. Prime minister of Italy from 1917 to 1919, he resigned after failing to win more territory for Italy at the Paris Peace Conference.

PHILIPPE PÉTAIN (1856–1951) Career French soldier who achieved prominence in organising the defence of Verdun in 1916. He was appointed French commander-in-chief in 1917 amidst serious mutinies and successfully restored order. He came out of retirement in 1940 to become prime minister and signed the armistice with Hitler's Germany. He then was head of state of Vichy France until 1944.

GAVRILO PRINCIP (1894–1918) Bosnian Serb who joined the Serb nationalist organisation the Black Hand and assassinated the Archduke Franz Ferdinand, heir to the Austro-Hungarian Empire, in Sarajevo in June 1914. He died in prison from tuberculosis.

ANTONIO SALANDRA (1853–1931) Italian conservative politician who held several cabinet posts before the First World War. Prime minister from 1914 to 1916, Salandra took Italy in to the First World War in 1915 as an ally of Britain and France. He resigned in 1916.

ALFRED VON SCHLIEFFEN (1833–1913) German career soldier, chief of staff from 1891 to 1905. He developed a plan for a decisive six-week offensive against France in the west before turning east to deal with the Russians. This was finalised in 1905 and became known as the Schlieffen Plan.

ALFRED VON TIRPITZ
(1849–1930)

Career sailor, appointed by Wilhelm II as secretary of state for the navy in 1897, a position he held until he retired in 1916. He was responsible for Germany's massive shipbuilding programme from 1898 onwards, which led to a naval race with Britain.

KAISER WILHELM II
(1859–1941)

King of Prussia, emperor of Germany from 1888 to 1918, and head of the Hohenzollern dynasty. He promoted the policy of '*Weltpolitik*', which aimed to make Germany a world power with a powerful navy and enlarged overseas territories. He abdicated in November 1918 and fled to Holland. Germany became a republic on Wilhelm's abdication.

WOODROW WILSON
(1856–1924)

Democratic politician and 28th President of the USA from 1913 to 1921. Wilson took the USA into the First World War in 1917. He published a set of peace proposals in 1918 known as 'the Fourteen Points'. At the Paris Peace Conference in 1919, Wilson advocated for lenient treatment of Germany and was pivotal in the establishment of the League of Nations. Despite Wilson campaigning hard for US membership, the Senate rejected US entry into the League of Nations.

1. THE CAUSES OF THE FIRST WORLD WAR

TOPICS

The assassination at Sarajevo
The unification of Germany
The alliance system
The formation of the Triple Entente
Colonial rivalry, *Weltpolitik* and the Anglo-German naval race
The arms race
The Schlieffen Plan
Balkan nationalism and great power rivalries in the Balkans
The July Crisis

Overview

This chapter examines the causes of the First World War and the complex historiographical debates surrounding this topic, particularly the debates relating to German war guilt, which will prove valuable for a fuller appreciation of differing historical perspectives that essay answers should incorporate to access the top mark bands on Paper 2.

It addresses a range of long-term factors including the impact of German unification (1871), the alliance system, imperialism (colonialism), the arms race (both on land and sea), and tensions in the Balkans.

The chapter concludes by looking at the July Crisis of 1914, examining the reasons why the crisis emanating from the assassination at Sarajevo escalated into a general European war. Candidates need to show awareness of a range of factors in answering a question on the causes of wars but also should consider and reach a judgement on the relative importance of those factors.

TIMELINE

1871 — Germany is unified as a nation

1878 — The Congress of Berlin meets

1879 — The Dual Alliance treaty is agreed between Germany and Austria-Hungary

1881 — The Three Emperors' League is established by Germany, Austria-Hungary, and Russia

1882 — The Triple Alliance is formed by Germany, Austria-Hungary, and Italy

1887 — The Reinsurance Treaty is signed by Germany and Russia

1888 — Kaiser Wilhelm II's accession to the throne

1890 — Bismarck resigns; the Reinsurance Treaty lapses

1894 — The Russian-French Alliance is formed

1897 — Wilhelm II launches the policy of *Weltpolitik*

1898 — 1st German Naval Laws

1900 — 2nd German Naval Laws

1903 — King Peter I of Serbia's accession to the throne

1904 — The Entente Cordiale agreements are signed by France and Britain

1904–5 — The Russo-Japanese War

1905 — 1st Moroccan Crisis

1906 — The Algeciras Conference
The HMS *Dreadnought* is launched

1907 — Anglo-Russian Entente

1908 — Austria-Hungary announces the annexation of Bosnia-Herzegovina

1911 — 2nd Moroccan Crisis
Italy invades Tripoli

1912 — The Anglo-French Naval Agreement is signed
1st Balkan War

1913 — 2nd Balkan War
The Zabern Incident

JUN 1914 — Archduke Franz Ferdinand is assassinated

JUL 1914 — Germany offers a 'blank cheque' to Austria-Hungary
Austria issues an ultimatum to Serbia
Austria-Hungary bombards Belgrade
Russia begins mobilisation

AUG 1914 — Germany declares war on Russia
Germany declares war on France
Germany invades Belgium
Britain declares war on Germany

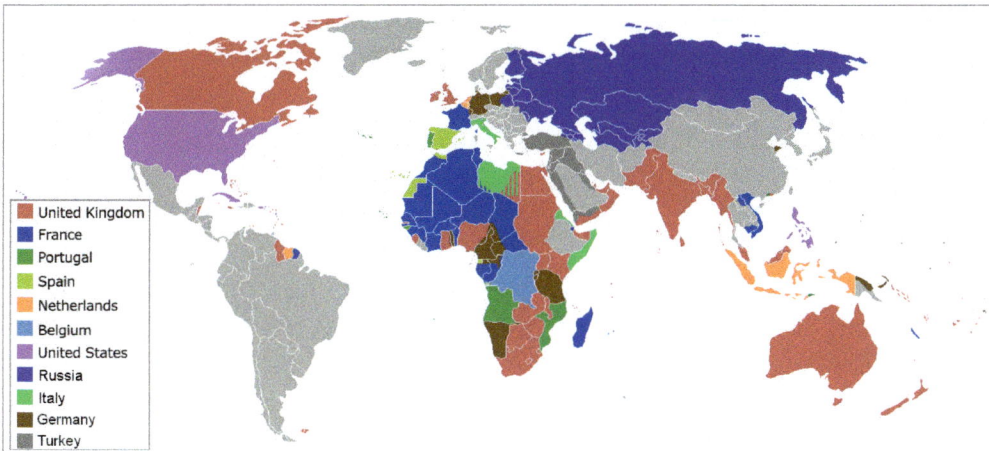

Figure 1.1: Map of major world powers in 1914

Source: Roke~commonswiki/ SpencerCS/Alvin Lee, via Wikimedia Commons. https:// commons.wikimedia.org/wiki/ File:Colonisation_1914.png (accessed 12 April 2018)

1.1 The Historical Debate about the Causes of the First World War

Perhaps no other question in history has aroused such fierce historical debate as the issue of who or what caused the First World War. Many historians have essentially accepted the verdict of Article 231 of the Treaty of Versailles (1919) that Germany and its allies were responsible for the outbreak of the war:

> The Allied and associated governments declare, and Germany accepts the responsibility for, all the loss and damage suffered by the Allied and associated governments as a consequence of the war imposed upon them by the aggression of Germany and her allies.

1.1.1 The Fischer Thesis

The most influential historian in this respect is Fritz Fischer who published two highly controversial works in the 1960s.

Fischer argues that:

- Germany had pursued an aggressive foreign policy since the 1890s aimed at expanding Germany's borders and that, from the time of the War Council meeting of December 1912, when senior figures in the German government discussed the likelihood of war in the near future, Wilhelm II's government wanted to go to war as soon as possible.

- The German government's expansionist aims of the pre–First World War period were very similar to those of the Nazis: that there was a basic continuity in German foreign policy between 1871 and 1939.

- The aggression of Wilhelm II's Germany was primarily motivated by the government's desire to strengthen its support among the German population, at a time when the power of the **Kaiser** and the German elites was being challenged by the growing strength of the **Socialists** who, by 1912, were the largest party in the **Reichstag**.

Historians who focus on domestic factors in shaping Germany's foreign policy see the Zabern Affair (1913) as highly significant. The Reichstag passed a vote of no confidence in Bethmann–Hollweg's government (by 293 to 54 votes) following the army's mistreatment of civilians in Zabern in **Alsace–Lorraine.** The government defended the

---

KEY TERMS

Kaiser: German term for 'Emperor'. Wilhelm II was Kaiser from 1888 to 1918.

Socialists: Politicians committed to ending inequalities in

wealth and transferring power from the Kaiser to the Reichstag.

Reichstag: Elected lower house of the German Parliament.

Alsace-Lorraine: Rich industrial region taken from France.

army's behaviour. Historians of the Fischer school see the Zabern Affair as highlighting the ongoing constitutional tensions in Germany which arguably made the prospect of a short, victorious war more attractive to the Kaiser and his advisers in 1914.

Fischer's thesis became the orthodox interpretation, replacing the view that had prevailed since the 1930s that no one country was responsible for the First World War and that, according to former British Prime Minister David Lloyd George, no country wanted war in 1914. Lloyd George saw the war as an accidental war, arguing that 'the nations in 1914 slithered over the brink into the boiling cauldron of war.'

Fischer's view that Germany deliberately engineered a war in 1914, to fulfil the aims of *Weltpolitik* (to make Germany a great imperial power), has received support from many historians, notably Immanuel Geiss and Ulrich Wehler. Geiss sees Germany as the aggressor in the July Crisis of 1914, putting pressure on Austria-Hungary to resolve by military action the threat posed by Serbia. According to Geiss, the government of Bethmann-Hollweg (German chancellor in 1914) was prepared to provoke a general European war to fulfil the aims of *Weltpolitik*.

1.1.2 Fischer's Critics

Fischer has many critics such as Gerhard Ritter. Ritter argues that:
- Germany acted defensively in July 1914 and was seeking a diplomatic victory over the Triple Entente of Britain, France and Russia, rather than a military one.

Other German historians, notably Egmont Zechlin, argue that:
- Germany in 1914 was seeking a preventative war, with no plans for acquiring land from its neighbours. They challenge Fischer's claim that Bethmann-Hollweg's September Programme (1914), in which the German government outlined possible war aims in terms of acquiring territory in Central Europe, reflects the German government's motives in going to war in 1914.
- The German government in the years immediately before the First World War was increasingly gloomy about the growing power of the Triple Entente of France, Russia, and Britain and went to war in desperation in 1914 as an attempt to break out of its 'encirclement' by the Triple Entente as the balance of power tipped increasingly in the favour of Germany's enemies. There is no doubt that the German government was more and more worried about the fragility of its chief ally, Austria-Hungary, which appeared menaced by the restless nationalism of its Slav subjects.

1.1.3 'War by Timetable'

A. J. P. Taylor (1969) argued that the war plans of the great powers were the chief cause of war in 1914. Taylor suggested that a diplomatic solution to the crisis following the assassination of the Archduke Franz Ferdinand, heir to the Austro-Hungarian Empire, proved impossible because the rival governments, believing that any war that broke out would be a short one and that military mobilisation speed would prove decisive, rushed to mobilise first. Once Russia announced its mobilisation at the end of July 1914, the German generals put their own government under intense pressure to either get Russia to cancel its mobilisation order or to begin German mobilisation. Within a few days all of the great powers had begun mobilisation.

🔑 **KEY TERMS**

Weltpolitik: The 'world' policy pursued by Wilhelm II from 1897 onwards, aimed at expanding Germany's overseas empire.

1.1.4 Marxist Interpretations

Lenin, the leader of the Russian **Bolshevik** Party, produced the most famous Marxist interpretation of the causes of the First World War in *Imperialism: The Highest Stage of Capitalism* (1916). The origins of the war, Lenin argued, lay above all else in the European great powers' race to expand their overseas empires in Africa and Asia in the late nineteenth and early twentieth centuries. Lenin saw these imperial rivalries as the result of capitalist competition for markets and resources.

Other Marxist historians have claimed that big businessmen and financiers shaped the foreign policies of the great powers before the First World War. However, Marxist interpretations fail to take into account that imperialism seems to have been driven much more by the search for prestige rather than profits. Similarly, Marxists have been unable to provide evidence to support their assertion that capitalist interests put pressure on European governments to go to war in 1914.

> **(?) KEY HISTORICAL PERSPECTIVES**
>
> **Summary of the historical debate about the causes of the First World War**
>
> | Fischer | Germany pursued an aggressive foreign policy and deliberately engineered the First World War in order to expand its territory and to strengthen the Geman government domestically. |
> |---|---|
> | Zechlin | The German government engineered a war in 1914 to escape what it saw as encirclement by the increasingly powerful Triple Entente. |
> | Taylor | The war plans of the Great Powers prevented a diplomatic solution to the July Crisis because all governments were obsessed with the importance of the speed of military mobilisation. |
> | Marxist historians | Colonialism/imperialism was the key factor in generating tensions between the Great Powers which led to war in 1914. |

1.2 The Assassination at Sarajevo: The Trigger for War

The event that triggered the outbreak of the First World War was the assassination of the Archduke Franz Ferdinand in Sarajevo (in Bosnia–Herzegovina) on 28 June 1914. The Archduke was heir to the Austro–Hungarian Empire, one of the great powers of Europe. He and his wife were shot dead by a Serb terrorist, Gavrilo Princip, while making a state visit to Bosnia–Herzegovina, which had only become officially part of the Austro–Hungarian Empire in 1908.

> **(➤) KEY ISSUES**
>
> **Why did the assassination at Sarajevo spark off a major war between the European great powers?**
>
> 1. Austria-Hungary decided to use the assassination as an excuse to go to war with Serbia: to crush it before Serbia became strong enough to attack Austria-Hungary. Many of the people living in the southern part of the Austro-Hungarian Empire were Slavs and the Austro-Hungarian government feared that Serbia might incite a rebellion by their Slavic subjects, threatening the break-up of Austria-Hungary. Princip was protesting at the occupation of Bosnia-Herzegovina by Austria-Hungary on the grounds that it contained many Serbs. Relations between Serbia and Austria-Hungary had become increasingly strained at the beginning of the twentieth century. ↳

> **KEY TERMS (➤)**
>
> **Bolshevik:** Political group committed to abolishing private property who seized power in Russia in 1917.

🔑 KEY ISSUES *(conitnued)*

2. Both Serbia and Austria-Hungary had close relations with other, powerful states, who became drawn into the conflict. Serbia had close diplomatic links with Russia, which in turn had signed alliances or agreements with France and Britain (this alliance between Russia, France, and Britain was known as the Triple Entente). Austria-Hungary was part of the Triple Alliance (Germany and Italy being the other two members). In July–August 1914 the members of the Triple Entente and Triple Alliance were, one by one (with the exception of Italy), drawn into the escalating conflict which had begun in the Balkans.

To understand why the First World War broke out it is necessary to consider why the two rival alliance systems emerged and why relations between the two groups of great powers deteriorated in the ten years or so before 1914.

1.3 The Impact of the Unification of Germany

Germany before the nineteenth century had not been a united country but rather a collection of several hundred different states. In the years 1862–71, Otto von Bismarck, the chancellor of Prussia (one of the largest German states), succeeded in uniting all of the German states into the German Empire.

Germany's unification transformed the balance of power in Europe as the German Empire was now the most powerful industrial and military state on the continent. Its population rose from 49 million to 66 million in the period 1890–1914 and its industrial output outstripped that of Britain to make Germany the leading industrial power in Europe. This was one reason why France and Russia signed a military alliance in 1894; both were neighbours of Germany and both, although great powers themselves, were worried about Germany's strength. Relations between Germany and France were poor throughout the period from 1871 to 1914 because the German states had defeated France in 1871 and Germany had taken the area known as Alsace-Lorraine from France. The French wanted Alsace-Lorraine back.

1.4 The Alliance System

Figure 1.2: Map of military alliances of Europe in 1914

Source: historicair (French original), Fluteflute and Bibi Saint-Pol (English translation), via Wikimedia Commons (CC BY-SA 2.5). https://commons.wikimedia.org/wiki/File:Map_Europe_alliances_1914-en.svg (accessed 12 April 2018)

The development of two rival alliance systems – the Triple Alliance and the Triple Entente – provided the mechanism by which a local conflict in the Balkans escalated into a general European war. However, that does not mean that the very existence of the alliances made war inevitable.

A. J. P. Taylor (1954) suggested that the alliances were so fragile that they should not be regarded as a major cause of the First World War:

> Yet it would be wrong to exaggerate the rigidity of the system of alliances or to regard the European war as inevitable. No war is inevitable until it breaks out. The existing alliances were all precarious. Italy was only the extreme example: it renewed the Triple Alliance and made exaggerated promises of military support to Germany on the one side, and sought to negotiate a Mediterranean agreement with France and Britain on the other. In France, the Russian alliance was increasingly unpopular; in June 1914, the British Government at last reached agreement with Germany over the Baghdad railway; and the French had already done so in February. Both seemed to be taking sides with Germany against Russia in the great question of Turkey-in-Asia

Taylor, 1954, p. 518

Furthermore, the existence of two powerful alliance systems could be seen as a deterrent, as a force for peace in that the European powers were acutely conscious that a quarrel between two of them could risk a general European war. Winston Churchill (1931) suggested this in his account of the First World War:

> The two mighty European [alliance] systems faced each other...with a tranquil gaze. A polite, discreet, pacific, and on the whole sincere diplomacy spread its web of connections over both. A sentence in a dispatch, an observation by an ambassador... seemed sufficient to adjust from day to day the balance of the prodigious structure... Were we after all to achieve world security and universal peace by a marvellous system of...armaments in equation, of checks and counter-checks on violent action ever more complex and delicate?

Churchill, 1931, p. 129

Nonetheless the alliance system can be seen as a key factor in understanding why war broke out because it did shape the war plans of the great powers, and these played a key role in the decisions made during the July Crisis in 1914. Historians like John Röhl argue that, by 1914, the German government was so alarmed that the balance of power was tipping decisively in favour of the Triple Entente that it was looking to either achieve a diplomatic victory by humiliating the Triple Entente following Franz Ferdinand's assassination or to fight a general European war while it was still strong enough to win.

1.4.1 Bismarck's Alliance System

Chancellor Bismarck of Germany's great preoccupation after 1871 was to keep France isolated so that it could not seek revenge for its defeat and the loss of Alsace-Lorraine to Germany in 1871. Bismarck wanted to ensure that Germany would always be '*à trois* in a Europe of five powers'. France on its own, Bismarck assumed, would not dare attack Germany. To keep France isolated, without allies, Bismarck signed a series of defensive military alliances:

- The Dual Alliance with Austria-Hungary in 1879
- The Three Emperors' Alliance with Austria-Hungary and Russia in 1881
- Germany also concluded the Triple Alliance with Italy (and Austria-Hungary) in 1882.

Bismarck increasingly struggled to keep Russia and Austria-Hungary together within the same alliance as their rivalry in the **Balkans** deepened. A new Balkan crisis over Bulgaria in 1885–86 saw Austria-Hungary's relations with Russia at breaking point and meant that there was no renewal of the Three Emperors' Alliance when it expired in 1887.

KEY TERMS

Balkans: Area in South Eastern Europe, so-called because of the mountain range running through it.

Bismarck therefore decided to try to keep on good terms with both Austria-Hungary and Russia by means of separate treaties:

- The Dual Alliance with Austria-Hungary continued to be renewed every five years.
- Bismarck also signed a separate agreement with Russia, the Reinsurance Treaty in 1887.

Yet this remained a very difficult juggling act for Bismarck and there were clear signs that Russo-German relations were under strain well before the accession of Kaiser Wilhelm II in 1888.

Wilhelm II wanted to follow very different policies from those of Bismarck. In 1890 Bismarck resigned and Wilhelm II did not renew the Reinsurance Treaty with Russia. Gradually, France and Russia drifted together to form an alliance in 1894. This meant that the nightmare, which Bismarck had dreaded had now come to pass: France had a powerful ally and Germany faced the potential threat of a simultaneous attack from both east and west.

Figure 1.3: 'Dropping the Pilot'. A caricature by Sir John Tenniel (1820–1914), first published in *Punch* magazine, March 1890

Source: Thomas L. Minnick Collection, The Ohio State University, Billy Ireland Cartoon Library & Museum. https://library. osu.edu/dc/concern/generic_ works/g7330j58d (accessed 3 April 2018)

DROPPING THE PILOT.

1.5 The End to Britain's 'Splendid Isolation' and the Formation of the Triple Entente

Until 1904 Great Britain avoided being drawn into military alliances or diplomatic engagements with any of the European powers. Britain believed its interests were best served by remaining in '**splendid isolation**,' free to concentrate on its vast overseas empire and commercial interests. However, after 1904 Britain was increasingly drawn into diplomatic ties: with France in 1904 and Russia in 1907.

Both the **Entente Cordiale** between Britain and France and the Anglo-Russian Entente originally were intended to reduce tensions created by imperial rivalries between the signatories: in the case of France and Britain this was principally in North Africa, while Russia and Britain were competing for influence in Afghanistan and Central Asia. However, these diplomatic understandings over time took on an increasingly anti-German nature, and, by 1914, the British government felt it could not stand by and see Germany defeat France. The main reason why Britain drew closer and closer to its Triple Entente partners was the alarm in Britain generated by the aggressive imperialism and naval expansion pursued by Kaiser Wilhelm II of Germany after 1897 under the policy known as *Weltpolitik*. Britain was primarily concerned by the threat that Germany appeared to pose to its overeas empire.

1.6 Colonial Rivalry, *Weltpolitik* and the Anglo-German Naval Race

Between 1870 and 1900, Britain, France, Germany, Belgium and Italy were all involved in the so-called 'Scramble for Africa' and a search for influence and territory in the Far East, at the expense of China.

Africa
By 1880, 10% of Africa had been taken over by European states; by 1900, 90% had been.

Asia
The Chinese Empire was in serious decline. After the Opium Wars of the 1840s, Great Britain was given Hong Kong; Japan defeated China in 1895; Russia forced China to grant it a 25-year lease on the Liaotung Peninsula; and Germany occupied Kiaochow.

1.6.1 The Causes of Colonialism (Imperialism)

1. **Economic**
   Lenin argued that imperialism was driven by the interests of capitalists, seeking new markets and control of raw materials. However, European powers gained little in the way of raw materials from their colonies and colonial trade constituted only a small percentage of their overall trade.

2. **Nationalism**
   Colonies were seen as giving states prestige; imperialism was popular. There was a widespread belief in **Social Darwinism**; that is, the strongest states would expand at the expense of the weaker.

3. **Religious belief**
   Many Europeans saw it as their duty to bring civilisation and Christianity to the 'backward' peoples of Africa.

4. **Imperialism driven from below rather than by governments**
   The actions of European officials and businessmen in Africa were often responsible for colonial expansion, rather than the policies of governments.

KEY TERMS

Splendid Isolation: Term that was used to describe the Conservative Party's policy in the second half of the nineteenth century of keeping Britain out of any entangling alliances. The phrase is attributed to the Canadian politician, George Foster.

Entente Cordiale: French for 'friendly agreement'. Term by which the Anglo-French treaty was known. It was not a military alliance but a diplomatic understanding.

Imperialism: Policy whereby a country seeks to expand its territory to create an empire outside its existing borders. In the nineteenth and early twentieth centuries, several European powers competed in acquiring larger and larger overseas empires.

Nationalism: Pride and belief in promoting the strength of one's own country, putting its interests first, even if at the expense of other countries.

Social Darwinism: The application of Charles Darwin's theory of the 'survival of the fittest' to the human species. In the nineteenth century there was a widespread belief that nations had to either survive through expansion or risk declining and being taken over by stronger nations.

🔑 **KEY ISSUES**

What was the impact of imperialism on international relations?

- It led to growing tension between Britain and France in the late nineteenth century; notably seen in the Fashoda Incident of 1898 when French and British troops confronted each other in the Sudan.
- It led to growing tension between Britain and Russia over the Far East and Central Asia.
- It led to the Russo-Japanese War (1904–5); Russia's defeat resulted in it turning its attention back to the Balkans and this contributed to increasing international tension in the decade before 1914.
- The Russo-Japanese War directly led to the Entente Cordiale between Britain and France in 1904. Britain was allied to Japan (1902) and France was an ally of Russia (1894). Both countries were worried that they might be dragged into the Russo-Japanese War, so they signed the Entente Cordiale to minimise this risk and also to resolve long standing colonial disagreements, for example, over Morocco and Egypt. Although this agreement was not an alliance and was not aimed against Germany, it worried Germany and contributed to its fear of encirclement.
- Arguably colonialism provided a safety valve for the European states where their rivalry might cause tension but never reached the point that war was likely.
- It encouraged the development in Germany of *Weltpolitik* and this did contribute to heightened international tension, particularly after 1905.

1.6.2 German *Weltpolitik*

Chancellor Bismarck of Germany had had little interest in acquiring colonies, although he did indulge the German public by seizing territories in south–west, west and east Africa in the mid–1880s. However, Kaiser Wilhelm II was very keen to make Germany into a world power; he was jealous of Britain and felt that Germany needed a large colonial empire to be regarded as a great power.

Von Bulow (the German foreign minister) famously articulated this sentiment in 1897:

> We don't want to put anyone else in the shade, but we too demand a place in the sun.

Quoted in Henig, 1993, p. 10

Wilhelm launched *Weltpolitik* in 1897, committing Germany to the acquisition of more colonies and to the building of a powerful navy. The main architects of *Weltpolitik* were Klaus von Bulow and Alfred von Tirpitz, respectively appointed in 1897 as foreign minister and naval minister. Both saw *Weltpolitik* as an important instrument for rallying support for the imperial government, promoting patriotism and weakening the Socialists who were critical of imperialism and increased spending on armaments. The German Navy League and the Pan–German League campaigned in support of *Weltpolitik*. Wilhelm was very disappointed with the results of his policy in that very little was acquired in terms of further colonies.

However, Wilhelm's attempt to promote Germany's influence overseas had important consequences:

- It created considerable friction with the leading colonial powers, chiefly Great Britain and France, and helped bring Britain out of its traditional 'splendid isolation' in the search for closer links with France and Russia.
- In turn, this led Germany increasingly to see itself as encircled by the Triple Entente of Great Britain, France, and Russia.

1.6.3 The First and Second Moroccan Crises (1905–6 and 1911)

Both of these crises saw the German government acting aggressively in an attempt to increase its influence in North Africa. In doing so, Germany pushed France and Britain closer together, thereby increasing Germany's fear of encirclement.

The First Moroccan Crisis (1905–6)

In 1905 the Kaiser visited Tangier to announce Germany's commitment to the continuing independence of Morocco, which was part of the Ottoman (Turkish) Empire but which several European countries had commercial interests in. The Kaiser's visit was meant to signal to France that it could not increase its influence in Morocco without prior consultation with Germany. The German government expected Britain to fail to support France and hoped the Entente Cordiale (1904) would then collapse. In fact, Germany's attempt to bully France did the opposite as Britain and France stood together at the Algeciras Conference (1906), which was called to resolve the dispute.

The Second Moroccan Crisis (1911)

In 1911 the German government sent the gunboat SMS *Panther* to the port of Agadir in protest at France's decision to send more troops to Morocco. Britain reacted strongly, fearing Germany was seeking to acquire a naval base in the Mediterranean. David Lloyd George, the British chancellor of the exchequer, made a thinly veiled threat of war in his Mansion House speech.

Although the crisis fizzled out with France and Germany agreeing to increased French influence in Morocco in return for France handing over territory in the Congo to Germany, a lot of damage was done to international relations:

- France and Britain's suspicions about Germany's intentions were strengthened.
- 1912 saw France and Britain sign an important naval agreement involving the two countries cooperating in their naval deployments in the North Sea and Mediterranean.

1.6.4 German Naval Expansion

Figure 1.4: The German High Seas Fleet

Source: The Great War Primary Documents Archive, via Wikimedia Commons. https://en.wikipedia.org/wiki/File:Hochseeflotte_1.jpg (accessed 10 April 2018)

Germany's growing middle class was very eager to see Germany build a large navy. The German government supported this partly as a way of rallying patriotic feeling and because Wilhelm II believed a powerful fleet was essential if Germany were to become a great colonial power.

In 1898 and 1900, the Reichstag passed the First and Second Naval Laws, drawn up by Tirpitz, which greatly expanded the German Navy; under the First Naval Law, three battleships were to be built every year for the next 20 years.

Britain believed that it had to maintain its position as the world's greatest naval power to defend both Britain itself and its vast overseas empire. At first, Britain was not seriously alarmed by the German naval programme as it had such a huge lead over Germany: in 1898 Britain possessed 38 first-class battleships to Germany's seven.

However, from 1906 the situation was transformed and a full-scale Anglo-German naval race developed. This followed on the construction of a revolutionary new battleship, the HMS *Dreadnought*, which was immediately copied by the Germans (the *Nassau* class). The *Dreadnought* made all previous battleships virtually obsolete, and, in the years up to 1912, Germany was more or less neck-and-neck with Britain in the race to build Dreadnoughts. 1906 also saw Germany announce plans to widen the Kiel Canal to allow *Dreadnought*-class ships pass from the Baltic to North Sea.

From 1912 Britain was able to outstrip Germany in construction of Dreadnoughts as Germany reduced its naval spending to increase spending on its army. In spite of this, the naval race, alongside Germany's aggressive behaviour during the Moroccan Crises, soured Anglo-German relations and helped cement the Triple Entente.

Sir Edward Grey, the British foreign secretary, made this clear in a speech made in February 1906:

> If there is a war between France and Germany, it will be very difficult for us to keep out of it. The Entente and still more the constant and emphatic demonstrations of affection...have created in France a belief that we shall support them in war. If this expectation is disappointed, the French will never forgive us. There would also I think be a general feeling that we had behaved badly and left France in the lurch.

Quoted in Joll and Martel, 2007, p. 65

1.6.5 German Fear of Encirclement

As well as the Entente Cordiale of 1904, Britain had also signed an Entente with Russia in 1907, in an attempt to reach an agreement over disputes concerning Afghanistan and the Near East. This was not a military alliance but Germany's aggressive behaviour strengthened relations between Russia and Britain. This, in turn, led German politicians to become increasingly worried about encirclement by the Triple Entente.

Kaiser Wilhelm II and his chancellor, Bethmann-Hollweg, were also very anxious about the possible collapse of Austria-Hungary as a great power. This was because Austria-Hungary was a multi-national empire and several of the nationalities within the empire were demanding greater independence. By 1914, the German government was frightened that Austria-Hungary might break up, leaving Germany alone to face the Triple Entente because Germany felt its other ally, Italy, was unreliable and weak too.

By 1914, the German government (and other countries too) believed a European war would break out sooner or later; in July 1914, they calculated that it would be better to go to war then rather than wait until later when Austria-Hungary was weaker and the Triple Entente stronger.

1.7 The Arms Race

> **KEY HISTORICAL PERSPECTIVES**
>
> **The historical debate about the significance of the arms race**
>
> Historians disagree about how significant the arms race between the great powers in the period before 1914 was in causing the First World War. Michael Howard argues that the arms race, which reflected the rival alliances, generated huge tensions and mutual suspicion that led to deteriorating international relations and explain the great powers' resort to war in the July Crisis in 1914. Howard (1970) also points out that the war plans drawn up by the great powers assumed that mobilisation speed would be decisive:
>
> > Millions of men had to be recalled to the colours, organized into fighting units, equipped with a vast apparatus of arms and services and sent by railways to their points of concentration, all within a few days. The lesson of 1870 [Prussia's swift victory against France] was burnt into the mind of every staff officer in Europe: the nation which loses the mobilization race is likely to lose the war...
> >
> > Quoted in Wolfson and Laver, 1996, p. 183
>
> However, recently Niall Ferguson has questioned whether increased military spending made the great powers more inclined to go to war, pointing out that, in the period immediately before the First World War, it was Britain who increased its expenditure most and that it was definitely not seeking war in 1914.
>
> Nonetheless, it is clear that there was a huge growth in the size of the armed forces of the great powers between 1890 and 1914:
>
> - France by 68% to 910,000 troops
> - Russia by 100% to 1,352,000 troops
> - Germany by 77% to 891,000 troops.
>
> Any increase by the French or Russians almost invariably triggered similar expansion by the Germans and vice versa.
>
> What is equally evident is that the arms race speeded up in the period 1910–14:
>
> - From 1908, Russia modernised and expanded its army, so that, by 1914, regulars and reservists together numbered six million
> - Germany's combined regulars and reservists totalled 4.5 million in 1914.
>
> One explanation for Germany's apparent readiness to risk a general European war in the summer of 1914 was its alarm at the growing might of the Russian Army; the German government viewed a possible European war as a way of breaking out of their encirclement by the Triple Entente and fighting Russia before her military reforms were completed (scheduled for 1917).

1.8 The Schlieffen Plan

Figure 1.5: Map of the Schlieffen Plan

Source: Courtesy of the USMA, Department of History. https://www.usma.edu/history/SiteAssets/SitePages/World%20War%20I/WWOne03.pdf (accessed 23 May 2018)

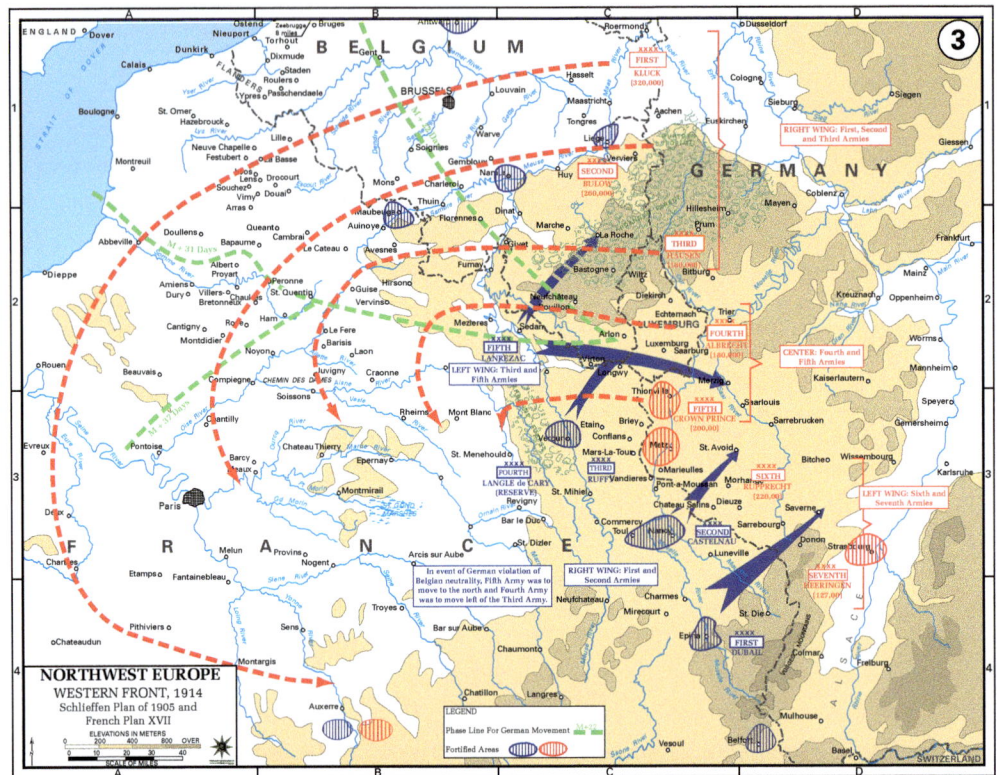

From 1891 to 1906, the chief of the German general staff was Count von Schlieffen. He saw a simultaneous French–Russian attack as the main threat to Germany's security and so devised a plan to counter this danger. In essence, his plan was:

- To knock out France within six weeks
- Then quickly transfer the bulk of the German armies east to face the Russians.

Schlieffen assumed that the technologically backward Russians would take about six weeks to mobilise their armies so that Germany would not face a major Russian attack while (initially) the majority (85%) of Germany's troops were attacking France. When von Schlieffen considered how to invade France, he concluded that most of Germany's troops should attack through Belgium, and a few through Holland. This was designed to avoid the very strong French fortresses on the Franco-German border between Belgium and Switzerland.

In 1906, Count von Moltke became chief of the German general staff and altered the Schlieffen Plan a bit. The most important change was that the German Army would not advance through Holland. However, it must be noted that Belgium was a neutral country, whose independence had been guaranteed by the great powers of Europe in a treaty dating back to 1839.

Table 1.1: Military and naval personnel of the great powers: 1890–1914

	1890	1900	1910	1914
France	542,000	715,000	769,000	910,000
Great Britain	420,000	624,000	571,000	532,000
Russia	677,000	1,162,000	1,285,000	1,352,000
Germany	504,000	524,000	694,000	891,000

1.9 Balkan Nationalism and Great Power Rivalries in the Balkans

> **KEY ISSUES**
>
> **Why do historians see the Balkans as such a key long-term cause of the First World War?**
>
> A power vacuum developed in South Eastern Europe, as the Ottoman Empire declined, which gave rise to great power competition to fill it. This, combined with growing Balkan nationalism, created dangerous tensions and appeared to threaten the survival of the Austro-Hungarian Empire.

Bosnia–Herzegovina, where the Archduke Franz Ferdinand was assassinated in 1914, had once been part of the Turkish (or Ottoman) Empire. From the fifteenth century, the Ottoman Turks had controlled virtually the whole of South Eastern Europe, the Middle East, and much of North Africa.

From the beginning of the nineteenth century, the Turkish Empire was in serious decline and a number of subject peoples, who were mainly Christian, broke away and became independent:

- The Greeks were the first to break away; an independent Greece was set up in 1830.
- In 1856, following the Crimean War, Rumania, Serbia and Bulgaria gained self-government within the Turkish Empire; and in 1878, following the Russo–Turkish War of 1877–78 and the Congress of Berlin, all of them gained full independence.

> **AUTHOR'S TIP**
>
> The country that is now spelled as 'Romania' was prior to the Second World War usually spelled as 'Rumania'.

As the Turkish Empire began to break up, the European great powers became increasingly involved in a struggle to acquire as much influence or land as possible, like vultures circling the 'sick-man of Europe' as the Turkish Empire known was commonly referred to, following Tsar Nicholas I of Russia's use of the phrase. The two European powers most interested in extending their influence in the Balkans were Austria–Hungary and Russia. Both empires bordered the Turkish Empire. Russia saw itself as the protector of the Slavs in this region and **Pan-Slavism** was influential in Russia, especially in the 1870s/80s. Russia also wanted to acquire a warm-water port and aimed to control the Straits of the Dardanelles, the narrow waterway that connects the Black Sea to the Aegean Sea. Austria–Hungary was suspicious of Russia's ambitions and sought to extend its own empire into Bosnia–Herzegovina. The Congress of Berlin (1878) gave Austria–Hungary the right to administer Bosnia–Herzegovina but the provinces remained officially part of the Turkish Empire.

BALKAN TROUBLES

THE BOILING POINT.

Figure 1.6: Balkan Troubles cartoon, 1913

Source: New Zealand History (Ministry for Culture and Heritage), via Wikimedia Commons. https://nzhistory.govt.nz/media/photo/balkan-troubles-cartoon (accessed 10 April 2018)

> **KEY TERMS**
>
> **Pan-Slavism:** Belief in the solidarity and unity of the Slavic peoples across Eastern Europe; Pan-Slavs in Russia believed that Russia had the duty to protect their fellow Slavs living within the Ottoman and Austro-Hungarian Empires.

1.9.1 Bismarck and the Balkans

Chancellor Bismarck believed that no German interests were at stake in the Balkans but he was very worried about the impact of the Balkans on Austria–Hungary's relations with Russia. His great fear was that Balkan tensions would prevent him from keeping both Austria and Russia friendly with Germany and that the result might be France acquiring an ally. Bismarck used diplomatic means to try to contain Balkan tensions – for example, his role as 'honest broker' at the Congress of Berlin (1878), where he tried to refrain from taking sides, and the signing of the Three Emperors League (1881) – but he would not support unconditionally Austria–Hungary's interests in the Balkans. He once remarked that the whole of the Balkans was not 'worth of the bones of a single Pomeranian musketeer'.

Figure 1.7: The Balkans in the late nineteenth century

Source: Courtesy of the University of Texas Libraries, the University of Texas at Austin. https://legacy.lib.utexas.edu/maps/historical/balkan_boundaries_1914.jpg (accessed 10 April 2018)

1.9.2 Balkan Crisis One: The Annexation of Bosnia-Herzegovina (1908)

From 1897 to 1905 Russian–Austrian rivalry over the Balkans was less fierce, partly because Russia was more interested in expanding its empire into the Far East. However, after 1905, when Russia was humiliatingly beaten in a war by Japan, Russia turned its attention back to the Balkans.

Another very important development occurred in 1903 when there was a change in the ruling dynasty in Serbia; up until 1903, Serbia's ruling family, the Obrenovich dynasty, had been quite friendly towards Austria–Hungary but, following the assassination of King Alexander, the Karageorgevic family took the throne and were much more pro-Russian and anti-Austrian.

In 1908 a very serious crisis broke out involving Serbia, Russia, Austria–Hungary, and Germany. Austria–Hungary had occupied the provinces of Bosnia and Herzegovina since 1878 but the area had technically remained part of the Turkish Empire. In 1908 Austria–Hungary announced that it was formally taking over Bosnia–Herzegovina, incorporating the provinces into its empire. This led to a major row with Serbia because:

- Serbia was an independent Balkan country which had its eyes on Bosnia-Herzegovina because there were many Serbs living there and because possession of Bosnia-Herzegovina would give Serbia access to the sea.

- Russia protested at Austria-Hungary's action because she did not want to see Austrian influence increase and also because Russia had a close relationship with Serbia (the Serbs and Russians were both Orthodox Christian in religion and were both Slavic peoples).

The crisis ended when Germany, Austria-Hungary's ally, forced Russia to back down by threatening her with war. Russia could not consider going to war in 1908 as she was still recovering from a serious revolution in 1905 and from the defeat by Japan.

What were the results of the crisis?

- Austria-Hungary kept Bosnia-Herzegovina.
- Relations between Austria-Hungary, on the one hand, and Serbia and Russia, on the other, deteriorated seriously.
- The Bosnian Crisis revealed a major change in German policy as Germany became increasingly interested in expanding its influence in the Balkans.

1.9.3 Balkan Crisis Two: The Balkan Wars (1912–13)

⧗ TIMELINE	
1911	Turkish power is further undermined when Italy invades Tripoli; this new demonstration of Ottoman weakness seems to encourage the formation of the Balkan League, comprising Bulgaria, Serbia, Greece and Montenegro
1912	The Balkan League attacks the Turkish Empire in the first Balkan War; they defeat Turkey and take a considerable amount of land from her
1913	The four members of the Balkan League fall out over who is to get which part of the land seized from the Turks; in this Second Balkan War, Serbia emerges as the main victor

What were the results of the Second Balkan War?

- Serbia doubled its territory and population.
- This alarmed Austria-Hungary which was fearful that the increasingly powerful and ambitious Serbia would try to stir up rebellion among Austria's Slav subjects in the south of her empire. Serbia appeared to threaten the future existence of the Austro-Hungarian Empire.
- One area that Serbia occupied in 1913 was Albania (formerly part of the Turkish Empire) and it only evacuated its troops from there under pressure from Austria-Hungary and Germany. Albania became an independent state.
- Once more Serbia's ally, Russia, had been humiliated as it stood by as Germany and Austria-Hungary had forced Serbia to back down.

Further friction between the great powers followed in October 1913 when Germany reached an agreement with Turkey whereby General Liman von Sanders was sent to assist in reforming the Turkish Army. Russia saw this as evidence of German interference in the region and protested bitterly; France and Great Britain joined in trying to force the German government to back down, which it duly did and Sanders was withdrawn in January 1914.

1.9.4 Balkan Crisis Three: The Sarajevo Assassination (June 1914)

The terrorist gang responsible for Franz Ferdinand's murder was the Black Hand, which had links with the Serbian government. The Austro-Hungarian government decided to use the assassination as an excuse to take strong action against Serbia but consulted its ally Germany first.

The 'Blank Cheque'

On 5 July, Kaiser Wilhelm II gave Austria–Hungary the so-called 'blank cheque': a promise to support Austria–Hungary fully in whatever action it took against Serbia.

KEY ISSUES

What did Germany intend in issuing the Blank Cheque?

- The German government realised that by urging Austria-Hungary to attack Serbia it was running the risk of sparking off a full-scale European war. Germany appears to have hoped that Russia would not come to Serbia's aid but rather would stand by and see Austria-Hungary crush Serbia; this would have strengthened Austria-Hungary (Germany's only reliable ally) and weakened Russia's prestige (and, therefore, that of the Triple Entente).

- However, Chancellor Bethmann-Hollweg clearly realised that it was much more likely that Russia would declare war on Austria-Hungary if it attacked Serbia. This would almost certainly bring all of the great powers into a general war. Germany was prepared to run this risk because they felt war would come sooner or later and calculated the war would be short and victorious.

Armed with an assurance of German support, on 23 July Austria–Hungary sent a harsh ultimatum to Serbia which it anticipated Serbia would reject, providing Austria–Hungary with an excuse to go to war. The historian Samuel Williamson notes that the July Crisis saw a 'fateful meshing of aggressive German *Weltpolitik* with an even more aggressive, irresponsible Habsburg Balkanpolitik'.

J. R. Western (1965) explains very clearly the concerns felt by Austria–Hungary and Germany about the very survival of the Habsburg Empire:

> The war of 1914 was due to the unbearable national tensions within Austria-Hungary and the attempt of that power to escape from them by action dangerous to peace. The continued existence of the **Habsburg** monarchy as a great power was the thing at stake in the war, at least to start with.

Quoted in Western, 1965

Serbia actually accepted most of the demands but refused to allow Austria to send police into Serbia to investigate the assassination. This resulted in Austria–Hungary declaring war on Serbia on 28 July.

Figure 1.8: Satirical map of Europe on the eve of the First World War

Source: Library of Congress, LC-USZ62-21659.
http://www.loc.gov/pictures/item/2009631644 (accessed 10 April 2018)

1.10 The July Crisis: A Balkan Conflict Escalates into a General European War

Once Austria–Hungary declared war on Serbia, the alliance system ensured that the conflict escalated into a general European war. All of the great powers expected the war to be over quickly and all, therefore, were under great pressure from their generals to mobilise as quickly as possible. This made a diplomatic solution to the crisis very unlikely.

KEY TERMS

Habsburg: The ruling family of the Austro-Hungarian Empire.

Austria-Hungary's declaration of war put Russia in a difficult position as the Russian government felt it could not stand by and see Serbia crushed because that would undermine Russian prestige and boost Austrian influence in the Balkans. However, if Russia ordered a general mobilisation of its armed forces this would inevitably prompt Germany to mobilise against Russia. Nicholas II hoped to be able to order just partial mobilisation against Austria-Hungary to put pressure on Austria-Hungary to cease its attack on Serbia. However, following Germany's ultimatum to Russia demanding the latter cancel its partial mobilisation, Nicholas reluctantly decided to order general mobilisation against both Germany and Austria-Hungary.

Austria-Hungary ordered a general mobilisation on 30 July. Germany responded on 31 July by sending an ultimatum to Russia demanding she stop mobilisation and then asked France what she would do in the event of war between Germany and Russia. Russia decided it could not be humiliated again by Germany and so continued to mobilise, therefore, on 1 August Germany declared war on Russia.

On 3 August, the French government informed Germany that she would be 'guided by her own interests' and so Germany declared war on France. On the same day, the German government began to put the Schlieffen Plan into operation and the German Army began to invade neutral Belgium. On 4 August, the British government decided to honour its guarantee of Belgium's neutrality and declared war on Germany. Up until Germany's invasion of Belgium, the British government seemed divided and uncertain about how to react to the impending European war. The German government seems to have hoped that Britain would remain neutral but believed that Britain's small army would be of no significance in terms of preventing the Schlieffen Plan from working. Britain's power was based on its navy but Germany was expecting a very brief war in which navies would play little or no part.

⧗ TIMELINE

The July Crisis of 1914

23 JUL	The Austrian ultimatum is sent to Serbia
25 JUL	Serbia replies to the ultimatum. Its reply is conciliatory but fails to satisfy Austria-Hungary which cuts off diplomatic relations with Serbia Tsar Nicholas II orders preparations for the mobilisation of Russia's armed forces
26 JUL	Sir Edward Grey, the British foreign secretary, proposes an international conference of ambassadors to be held in London to discuss the crisis Austria-Hungary begins to mobilise her forces on Russia's border
27 JUL	France accepts Grey's proposal Austria-Hungary decides to declare war on Serbia Bethmann-Hollweg, the German chancellor, rejects Grey's proposal
28 JUL	Austria-Hungary declares war on Serbia and starts to bombard Belgrade, the Serbian capital Kaiser Wilhelm, at this stage, seems to become anxious at the apparent imminence of war with Russia and so appeals to the Austrian government to 'halt in Belgrade' and to use the Serbian reply of 25 July as a basis for negotiations Russia begins partial mobilisation
29 JUL	It is now Bethmann-Hollweg's turn to have second thoughts. He is alarmed that Grey announced that Britain would not remain neutral if a general European war broke out, and by the news that Russia had ordered a partial mobilisation, an action which brought the danger of general war much nearer ↳

⌛ **TIMELINE** *(continued)*

Only now does Bethmann-Hollweg try to moderate Austria-Hungary's policy by urging her to accept a British version of the 'Halt in Belgrade' solution whereby Austria-Hungary would occupy the Serbian capital as a pledge for the settlement of her demands. But, by now, it is too late

31 JUL

Bethmann-Hollweg tells Russia that, if it does not cancel its mobilisation, Germany will mobilise and declare war. Tsar Nicholas II had originally only ordered partial mobilisation as a means of bringing pressure to bear on Austria-Hungary, not to threaten Germany. However, on 31 July this becomes a general mobilisation. The Russian government decides it cannot climb down and be humiliated again

The German government asks France what she would do in the event of war between Germany and Russia

1 AUG

Russia refuses to stop mobilisation so Germany declares war on Russia

3 AUG

France informs Germany that she would be 'guided by her own interests.' Therefore, Germany declares war on France

Germany invades Belgium

4 AUG

Britain declares war on Germany because Britain had signed a treaty, dating from 1839, guaranteeing Belgian neutrality

2. THE COURSE OF THE FIRST WORLD WAR

Overview

This chapter examines the course of the fighting in the First World War, primarily on the so-called Western Front (Belgium and France) and Eastern Front (Russia) but also other fronts such as Gallipoli (the Ottoman Empire).

It starts by taking a chronological approach to the events of 1914–18, year by year, analysing the key developments throughout those years and summarising the reasons for Germany's surrender in 1918. The chapter then goes on to analyse the nature of the fighting in the First World War, examining the most important technological developments and how these shaped the course and nature of the fighting. It also considers the concept of 'total war', the total mobilisation of a country's human and economic resources to support warfare, and illustrates this in detail through cases studies of the home front in Britain and Germany during the war.

TIMELINE

The First World War

AUG 1914

Germany invades Luxembourg, Belgium, and France with 1.7 million troops
France launches **Plan XVII**: this leads to huge French casualties (300,000)
The British Expeditionary Force (BEF) arrives in France/Belgium; they delay the Germans at Mons
Russians mobilise quickly (within 19 days); Russian troops advance into East Prussia; Moltke transfers 60,000 German troops from the Western Front to the east
The Russian Army is defeated at Tannenberg

SEP 1914

The Russians are defeated at the Masurian Lakes
The Battle of the Marne: the French and the BEF push the Germans back to the Aisne
Moltke resigns and is replaced by Falkenhayn
'Race to the Sea': the Germans try to outflank the Allies
The Russians defeat Austrians at Lemberg

OCT 1914

The Ottoman Empire enters the war on the side of the **Central Powers**

OCT/NOV 1914

The Germans' flanking manoeuvre is thwarted by the BEF and the French at the First Battle of Ypres; trench lines are formed

APR 1915

The Second Battle of Ypres: the first use of poison gas by the Germans, but they fail to capture Ypres
'Weak-point strategy': the **Entente Powers** (including ANZACs) land troops at Gallipoli but fail to capture the peninsula: the Allies are pinned down at Gallipoli for rest of year

MAY 1915

Italy joins the Allies, after signing the Treaty of London with Britain and France
Major Austro-German offensive against the Russians: the Russians are driven out of Poland, Lithuania, and Latvia, and they suffer huge losses

SEP 1915

France launches an offensive in Champagne: they suffer 1.5 million casualties
Bulgaria joins the Central Powers

OCT 1915

Serbia is defeated by a combination of forces from Bulgaria, Austria-Hungary, and Germany
Britain and France land troops at Salonika (Greece) to help Serbia but are pushed back into Greece by the Bulgarians; Greece remains neutral

JAN 1916

Allies evacuate troops from Gallipoli

FEB 1916

Falkenhayn launches attack on Verdun, and seeks to 'bleed France white'
The Battle of Verdun lasts until December; the French hold out: 380,000 French casualties; 340,000 German casualties

MAY/JUN 1916

The Battle of Jutland: the only major clash between British and German navies; losses are even but the German Navy never attempts to break the British naval blockade again

↳

⧖ TIMELINE (continued)

JUN 1916
Brusilov offensive is launched by the Russians: they have great initial success against the Austrians (Galicia is taken; 350,000 Austrians are captured) but are eventually (in September) pushed back by the Germans with big Russian losses

JUL 1916
The biggest British offensive of the war to date; Field Marshal Haig tries to break the German trench line on the Somme; there is some French support but much less than originally planned. There are 60,000 British casualties on day one; the Somme develops into a battle of attrition: the total casualties at the end of the battle are 400,000 British, 400,000 German, and 200,000 French

AUG 1916
Rumania joins the Allies (they want to gain Transylvania from Hungary)

NOV 1916
The Battle of the Somme ends: the British have gained very little ground

DEC 1916
Rumania is forced to surrender by the Bulgarians, Germans, and Austro-Hungarians

JAN 1917
Germany announces unrestricted submarine warfare
The USA learns of the Zimmerman Telegram by which Germany secretly tried to get Mexico to declare war on the USA

FEB 1917
The Germans voluntarily pull their front line back on Western Front to the Hindenburg Line

FEB/MAR 1917
Revolution in Petrograd: Nicholas II abdicates
The new Provisional Government decides to continue the war

APR 1917
The USA declares war against the Central Powers
New French commander-in-chief, Robert Nivelle, launches a major French offensive: it is a disastrous failure and sparks major mutinies; Neville is replaced by Pétain who restores order but the French are unable to take the offensive for some time
Canadians capture Vimy Ridge, a strategic high point in Arras region

JUN 1917
After detonating huge mines, the British capture Messines Ridge, outside Ypres

JUL 1917
Haig launches the Third Battle of Ypres (Passchendaele): he seeks a quick breakthrough but stalemate ensues; Passchendaele becomes known as the 'battle of the mud'; it results in 500,000 British and British Empire casualties; the Battle ends in November

OCT 1917
The Battle of Caporetto: a huge setback for the Italian Army, as they lose 500,000 troops as a result of an Austro-German offensive

NOV 1917
Bolshevik Revolution in Russia
The Battle of Cambrai: the massed British tanks breakthrough but achieve only temporary gains as their infantry are unable to follow up and the Germans counter-attack

DEC 1917
Bolshevik Russia signs ceasefire with Germany
The Germans are able to transfer troops to the Western Front but have to leave one million in the east because they seek major territorial gains there

JAN 1918
President Wilson announces his Fourteen Points

MAR 1918
The Treaty of Brest-Litovsk: Germany imposes harsh terms on Russia which is forced to hand over Poland, the Baltic region, Georgia, and the Ukraine
Ludendorff launches Operation Michael: storm troopers are used to break-through on the Western Front: the Germans advance 40 miles on the Somme

TIMELINE *(continued)*	
APR 1918	The second German offensive breaks through south of Ypres
MAY 1918	The third German offensive breaks through and reached Soissons.
JUL 1918	The Germans reach and cross the Marne but the Allies counter-attack and drive the exhausted Germans back
AUG 1918	A massive British counter-offensive at Amiens is met with great success; they advance eight miles The 'Hundred Days' of Allied counter-attacks begins German resistance begins to crumble
SEP 1918	American troops capture St Mihiel Allied troops move forward all along the Western Front Bulgaria surrenders after Allied advance from Salonika
OCT 1918	4th: Austria-Hungary and Germany ask President Wilson for an armistice on the basis of his Fourteen Points 28th: German Navy at Kiel mutinies 30th: Big Italian victory against the Austrians at Vittorio Veneto 30th: Turkey surrenders after British advances in Middle East
NOV 1918	3rd: Austria-Hungary surrenders 9th: Kaiser Wilhelm II abdicates: the German Republic is established 11th: Armistice ends the First World War

2.1 Overview of the Western Front in 1914–18

The enduring image of the First World War is of soldiers bogged down in trench fighting in Belgium and northern France, with minimal gains being made at the cost of very high casualties, as attacking infantry were mown down by machine gun and artillery fire. This stereotypical view, indeed, does reflect the reality of much of the fighting on the Western Front in Belgium and northern France where the Germans confronted the French, Belgians, British and, later, the Americans.

However, this picture requires important qualifications:

- First, although the First World War was not as global a conflict as the Second World War proved, there were many theatres of fighting: in Eastern Europe where the Russians contested the Eastern Front with the Austrians and Germans; on the Austro–Italian border after Italy joined the war in 1915; in the Balkans where the Austrians, Germans, and Bulgarians attacked Serbia; in the Ottoman Empire where Turkey faced British and British Imperial Troops at Gallipoli; in Mesopotamia and the Middle East; and in Africa where the British attacked Germany's colonies.
- Second, while stalemate in which neither side made a significant advance did typify the Western Front for much of 1914–17, there was a war of movement in the opening months of the war and again from the spring of 1918.

2.2 1914

Rapid movement characterised the opening phase of the war in the west between August and October 1914. The Germans sought to knock out France in six weeks, putting into effect the Schlieffen Plan, and, in the first weeks of the war, the main German armies swept through Belgium into northern France as they sought to envelop the left flank of the French armed forces. Other German forces were stationed on the Franco–German border to hold up the anticipated French offensive as the French sought to regain Alsace-Lorraine, taken by Germany in 1871, and on Germany's border with Russia.

As Schlieffen had laid down, the main German focus was to be on France, against which seven German armies were deployed, with just one German army positioned to deal with any attack by the Russians; only when France was defeated would her forces be concentrated against the Russians.

The French, as soon as war broke out, implemented Plan XVII, in an attempt to retrieve Alsace-Lorraine from Germany. Meantime, the British mobilised the BEF and swiftly despatched it to France so that it could try to aid the French in repelling the German invasion.

In the east, Russia mobilised her vast armies as quickly as they could to relieve the German pressure on France, while Austria-Hungary's main focus was its attack on Serbia.

2.2.1 The Western Front: The Failure of the Schlieffen Plan

The German commander-in-chief in 1914 was Helmuth von Moltke. Before the First World War he had made two major changes to the Schlieffen Plan:

- First, he transferred more troops to Germany's eastern frontier in response to Russia's faster mobilisation capability as a result of its improved railway network.
- Second, in the west, Moltke positioned more troops on the left wing of the German forces, on the German border with France. Whereas Schlieffen had planned to station seven times as many troops on Germany's right flank (on Germany's border with Belgium) than the left, under Moltke, the ratio was just 3:1 in favour of the right, thus weakening the German advance into Belgium.

In August 1914 Germany invaded Luxembourg, Belgium, and France with between 1.5 million and 1.7 million troops.

KEY ISSUES

Why did the Schlieffen Plan fail in 1914?

A number of factors meant that the advance was slower than the timetable laid down under the Schlieffen Plan:

- The 120,000 soldiers of the BEF arrived in France much sooner than the Germans had thought possible and inflicted heavy casualties on the Germans at Mons.
- Belgian resistance was more resolute than the Germans had anticipated; and the further the Germans pushed forward, the more difficult it was to keep them supplied.
- In early September, as German forces came close to Paris, the most northerly army swung east, rather than west, of Paris and exposed the German flank to counter-attack by combined French and British forces at the Battle of the Marne, which began on 5 September. The Germans were obliged to pull away from Paris to the River Aisne. Moltke resigned and was replaced by Erich von Falkenhayn.

The opening weeks of the war were disastrous for France as the offensive launched under Plan XVII resulted in huge French casualties, with over 210,000 Frenchmen lost in the first month of the war. The French were held up by the Germans in the 'Battle of the Frontiers' and then driven back.

2.2.2 'The Race to the Sea'

Following the Battle of the Marne, there were a series of attempted outflanking manoeuvres by the two sides as the Germans, French and British headed north: this is usually and mistakenly known as the 'race to the sea'. By late October, the opposing armies ran out of room and arrived at the Channel. At the First Battle of Ypres, the BEF and the French prevented the Germans from capturing Ypres and outflanking them. Trench lines were formed and the town of Ypres became a **salient**, with the Germans controlling the high ground around it. The war of movement on the Western Front was now at an end and it would be over three years before the stalemate of trench warfare was broken.

🔑 KEY ISSUES

Why was neither side able to make a breakthrough on the Western Front in the years 1914–17?

The historian John Terraine (1975) explains very clearly why for so long neither side found it possible to restore movement on the Western Front:

> It was the Industrial Revolution which had produced the masses [of people]. It was the Industrial Revolution that made it possible to mobilise them, arm them, feed them, move them. This war, as no previous one, was dominated by technology. This was above all, a war of fire-power: the fire-power of artillery, and the fire-power of the new automatic weapons – magazine rifles and machine guns. Fire-power filled the air and saturated the ground with projectiles and deadly fragments. To avoid them, men went underground into trenches, dug-outs and reinforced concrete 'pill-boxes'. To protect these, they placed 'aprons' of barbed wire – thousands of miles of it.
>
> And thus they created an obstacle which only more intense fire-power could destroy…

Terraine, 1975, p. 132

By the end of 1914, the BEF had lost 96,000 men and the French 995,000, while German casualties totalled nearly 670,000. Although Germany was now tied down in a war on two fronts, its forces occupied a large part of northern France which contained much of France's industrial resources.

2.2.3 The Eastern Front

The Russians completely upset Germany's plans by mobilising far more quickly than Schlieffen had anticipated. By 17 August Russian troops had invaded Germany as two Russian armies advanced into East Prussia. This led Moltke to transfer 60,000 German troops from the Western Front to the east.

In the east, Field-Marshal Paul von Hindenburg and General Erich von Ludendorff commanded Germany's forces which overwhelmed the Russians at Tannenberg (August) and the Masurian Lakes (September). The Russian commanders had failed to effect a junction of their two armies and fatally transmitted uncoded messages, telegraphing their movements to the Germans. These victories secured Germany's eastern frontier and made the reputations of Hindenburg and Ludendorff, who later, in 1916, took over supreme command of Germany's war effort.

🔑 KEY TERMS

Salient: A piece of territory held by one side in a conflict that juts out into enemy territory and is surrounded by it on a number of sides.

The Western Front: The area of north-western Europe, chiefly, Northern France and Belgium, where much of the fighting in the First World War took place.

The Eastern Front: The area of Eastern Europe, chiefly on Russia's western borders, where much of the fighting in the First World War took place between Russia, Germany, and Austria-Hungary.

2.3 1915

2.3.1 The Western Front

The German Army was largely on the defensive on the Western Front in 1915 as Falkenhayn decided to concentrate on trying to defeat Russia in the east. The only significant German offensive on the Western Front in 1915 was in April at the Second Battle of Ypres where the Germans used poison (chlorine) gas for the first time. Exploiting the disarray caused by the gas attack, the Germans captured high ground to the north of Ypres, but Ypres remained in Allied hands.

The year 1915 saw a number of major French and British offensives, none of which substantially altered the front line, and all of which resulted in heavy casualties for both sides:

- Between December 1914 and March 1915, the French were engaged in a series of attacks in the Champagne region.
- In March, at the Battle of Neuve Chapelle, the British Army broke through the German front line but little ground was gained after a German counter-attack. There were 12,000 British casualties.
- Between May and November, the French made repeated, unsuccessful attempts to capture the strategically important Vimy Ridge, which had been occupied by the Germans in September 1914.
- In September both the British and the French launched offensives. At Loos the British attacked using poison gas but, after an initial breakthrough, the attack failed because their reserves had been held too far back from the front. The British suffered 50,000 casualties. Sir John French was replaced as British commander-in-chief by Field Marshal Douglas Haig. The French mounted attacks in both Champagne and Artois but only limited gains were made.

2.3.2 The Eastern Front

May (1915)
The Germans launched a huge offensive against Russia's North West Front; this resulted in the Russians being driven out of Poland, Lithuania and Latvia. General Brusilov felt obliged to withdraw Russian troops on the South West Front too, so all of Russia's forces were in retreat. One million Russians surrendered during 1915.

August (1915)
Tsar Nicholas took over as commander-in-chief, in spite of the pleas of his ministers not to. This decision was disastrous as Nicholas was now based at Army HQ at Mogilev. The result was bureaucratic confusion with the tsar in Mogilev; the tsarina, the ministers, and the Duma in Petrograd; and the war industries, all at loggerheads.`

2.3.3 'Weak-point Strategy': The Gallipoli Campaign

The year 1915 witnessed a major debate among British and French politicians and military commanders about whether they should focus their attention wholly on driving the Germans out of France and Belgium, as the so-called 'westerners' argued, or, as the 'easterners' advocated, whether they would be better off trying to knock out the

---

KEY TERMS 🔑

Duma: The Russian Parliament.

weaker elements of the Central Powers, namely Austria-Hungary and Turkey, which had joined the war on Germany's side in October 1914.

In 1915 the Allies mounted the Gallipoli Campaign as a way of weakening the Central Powers at a time of stalemate and heavy losses on the Western Front. However, continuing arguments about strategic priorities meant that only limited resources were allocated to it.

KEY ISSUES

What were the objectives of the Gallipoli Campaign?

- To seize control of the Straits of the Dardanelles that separated the Aegean Sea from the Black Sea, with the aim of defeating Turkey.
- To reduce the pressure on Russia – fighting against Germany, Austria-Hungary, and Turkey. Also, the Allies could then supply Russia much more easily by means of the Straits.

TIMELINE

The Gallipoli Campaign (1915–16)

MARCH	Eighteen Allied ships try to enter the Dardanelles but four are sunk when they run into mines and the attempt is abandoned. The month delay before landing British troops gives the Turks the opportunity to strengthen their defences in the Gallipoli peninsula
APRIL	British and ANZAC (Australian and New Zealand) forces land at Gallipoli. The British fail to capture the high ground and so are pinned down on the beaches by Turkish fire and remain so for the rest of year. Gallipoli becomes a battle of attrition just like the Western Front.
JANUARY	All Allied forces are evacuated. Of the almost 500,000 Allied troops who fought at Gallipoli, the total casualties are 265,000; Turkish casualties are 300,000.

2.3.4 Other Fronts and Significant Developments in 1915

In May Italy joined the Allies, after signing the Treaty of London with Britain and France in which Italy was promised Austrian territory in the event of an Allied victory. Although the Italian Army was to have an undistinguished record, fighting eleven indecisive battles on the Isonzo river, Italy's entry into the war made Austria-Hungary's position much worse as she was now engaged on three fronts.

In the Balkans, Bulgaria joined the Central Powers in October and helped Austria-Hungary and Germany defeat Serbia. Britain and France landed troops at Salonika in neutral Greece to help Serbia, but they were pushed back into Greece by the Bulgarians while Greece remained neutral until July 1917 when it joined the Entente Powers.

2.4 1916

2.4.1 The Western Front

The Battle of Verdun

In February Falkenhayn unleashed a massive German attack on Verdun. The aim was not to capture Verdun but to draw in as many French soldiers as possible to defend the strategically important city and in the process to 'bleed France white'. Falkenhayn's intention was to wear the French down in a battle of attrition.

Up to a point, Falkenhayn's plan worked, as General Pétain moved unit after unit up to Verdun in a desperate attempt to hold on to it, and, by the end of the battle, in December, France had suffered about 500,000 casualties. The following year saw large-scale French mutinies and it is clear that the struggle at Verdun had seriously undermined the French Army's resilience and morale. However, Falkenhayn failed in that German losses were on a similar scale to French, with 400,000 casualties. Falkenhayn was duly replaced as commander-in-chief by Paul von Hindenburg.

The Battle of the Somme

In 1915 the French and British governments agreed on a joint attack on the Somme in 1916. Originally, the British and French were to provide equal numbers of troops, but the German attack on the French at Verdun meant that the bulk of the troops used in the Somme offensive were British.

The British commander, Sir Douglas Haig, planned an allied attack on a scale so large that a decisive breakthrough of the German front line would at last be achieved, and the stalemate of 1914–15 ended. Haig was confident that, by concentrating an unprecedented artillery barrage lasting seven days on the German front line, few German defenders would be left alive and a rapid advance would be possible. In fact, 1,900,000 shells were fired on the German trenches. However, about one million of the shells were shrapnel and did very little damage to the German earthworks because they were only filled with light steel balls, and only achieved a little more damage to the barbed wire; many shells failed to go off due to faulty fuses.

Due to the failure of the British artillery barrage and the inexperience of many of the British troops, the first day of the Somme proved to be the costliest in British military history with over 60,000 casualties. Haig continued with the attack until November, by which time there were 650,000 Allied casualties and 500,000 German. Tanks were used by the British for the first time in September in an attempt to deal with the barbed wire and trench defences; however, there were too few available to make a real impact and many broke down. At the end of the year, the Germans began to withdraw to a powerful system of new defences known as the Hindenburg Line.

2.4.2 The Eastern Front

General Brusilov launched a massive Russian offensive, with great initial success, against the Austrians in Galicia with 350,000 Austrians captured. However, in September the Russians were pushed back by the Germans with huge Russian losses and a serious decline in morale among the Russian troops.

2.4.3 Other Developments in 1916

In August Rumania joined the Allies because it wanted Transylvania from Austria-Hungary. However, within six months, Rumania withdrew from the war after a joint attack by Bulgarian, German and Austro-Hungarian forces.

2.5 1917

> ### 🔑 KEY ISSUES
>
> **What was Germany's strategy in 1917?**
> - By 1917, Germany's leaders were convinced that the collapse of Russia was imminent and that, with troops thus released from the Eastern Front, Germany could launch a massive attack in the West to defeat France and Britain.
> - To increase the pressure on the Entente Powers and starve Britain of supplies, on 8 January Germany announced unrestricted submarine warfare, having ↳

suspended its earlier campaign in 1915 after the *Lusitania* was sunk, with the loss of more than a hundred American lives. The U-boat (submarine) campaign hit the Allies very hard: between the end of 1916 and April 1917, Allied merchant shipping losses leapt from 350,000 tons a month to over 860,000 tons a month.

- The German government was well aware that unrestricted submarine attacks, which began in February, would mean American supply ships being sunk and that this would almost certainly provoke the USA into entering the war; however, it calculated that they could defeat the Entente powers before significant numbers of US troops arrived in Europe.

On 19 January the US government was informed by British cryptographers of the Zimmerman Telegram in which the German foreign minister (Zimmerman) instructed Germany's ambassador to Mexico to try to entice Mexico into an alliance against the USA, by offering it Texas, Arizona, and New Mexico in the event of Mexico declaring war on the USA. On 6 April the USA declared war on Germany.

2.5.1 The Western Front

Despite several major Allied offensives, fighting on the Western Front remained deadlocked in 1917.

⏳ **TIMELINE**

The Western Front (1917)

APRIL
⌄

A British offensive at Arras results in heavy casualties, although the Canadians distinguish themselves in capturing Vimy Ridge. The attack is launched in support of a big French offensive planned by Robert Nivelle, the French commander-in-chief. The offensive near St Quentin ends in disaster and is halted in May after about 100,000 French casualties. As a result, from late April, serious mutinies break out among many French units. Nivelle is replaced by Pétain who takes some time to restore discipline, by a mixture of firm action and improving conditions for the French soldiers. Consequently, the French are unable to mount a major offensive for the remainder of 1917.

Therefore, it falls to the British to keep the pressure on the Germans on the Western Front. Field Marshal Haig unleashes a series of offensives in Flanders, designed to drive the Germans away from the Ypres Salient and break through to the Belgian coast to seize the German U-boat bases at Ostend and Zeebrugge.

JUNE
⌄

The British general, Plumer, carries out a successful operation to capture the Messines Ridge, south of Ypres, after one million pounds of high explosives have been detonated under the ridge, destroying much of the German front line in that sector.

JULY
⌄

What is known as the Third Battle of Ypres, starting at the end of July, is characterised by a very costly series of British advances and it is not until November that the British capture the Passchendaele Ridge, still significantly short of the coastline. In the process, the British suffer about 250,000 casualties and the Germans at least 220,000.

NOVEMBER

The British mount a major offensive further south at Cambrai, deploying nearly 400 tanks. A five-mile breakthrough is temporarily achieved but, as with previous breakthroughs, it proves short-lived as the Germans successfully counter-attack.

2.5.2 The Austro-Italian Front

August 1917 saw the eleventh and final battle on the river Isonzo, with an Italian offensive against the Austrians failing to break the deadlock. However, in October, a major Austro-German victory was achieved at the Battle of Caporetto, when Italian forces were routed; the Italians suffered 700,000 casualties and many of their men deserted or were taken prisoner. Yet the Italians did manage to stabilise the front, so Caporetto did not prove decisive.

2.5.3 The Eastern Front

By 1917, 1.7 million Russians had been killed, eight million were wounded, and 2.5 million were prisoners. According to historian Norman Stone, the Russian Army was not on the point of collapse in 1917 but morale was poor, the Germans had captured much of western Russia, and the loss of many of the pre-war professional officers meant that discipline was starting to break down.

KEY ISSUES

What stresses did the war inflict on Russia's civilian population?

- As government spending increased by 800% between 1914 and 1916, it printed more paper money.
- Prices increased by 400% between August 1914 and March 1917.
- Severe food shortages affected the towns as 15 million peasants were called up to the armed forces and peasants started hoarding grain because they could not afford to buy manufactured goods at inflated prices.
- The fact that the transport network was focused on supplying the army's needs worsened the shortages.

The February Revolution

The fall of the Russian monarchy was not planned and took most people by surprise, including revolutionary groups like the Bolsheviks.

On 23 February demonstrations over bread shortages led to riots, which merged with a strike at the Putilov armaments factory. Many of the soldiers of the Petrograd garrison openly sided with the rioters. Rodzianko, the Duma president, contacted General Alexeyev, chief of the general staff. They agreed that the tsar's immediate abdication and the establishment of a new government were essential if order was to be restored.

On 2 March Nicholas II agreed to abdicate and Russia became a republic. The Duma chose ten of its members to serve as a temporary, Provisional Government, until elections could be held for a Constituent Assembly, which would draw up a new constitution.

The Provisional Government decided to continue the war. Alexander Kerensky, the war minister, launched a massive offensive in June 1917, but, by the first week in July, this had failed disastrously and morale among Russia's armed forces deteriorated sharply. The Provisional Government was no more successful in dealing with the social and economic problems caused by the war. By September, peasants across Russia were seizing land off the nobility. These seizures provoked growing desertions among the armed forces and further reduced food supplies; consequently, price inflation spiralled further out of control.

The October Revolution

Russia increasingly seemed on the verge of a second revolution and the political party that exploited this situation best was Lenin's Bolshevik Party. The German government had arranged for Lenin's return to Russia in a sealed train in April 1917, in the hope that he would cause trouble for the Russian government. Shortly after his return, Lenin delivered his April Theses, arguing that the Bolsheviks should prepare to overthrow the Provisional Government and promise to pull Russia out of the war. As the Provisional Government became increasingly unpopular, the Bolsheviks gained in support in Russia's major cities, and, in October (according to the Russian calendar which was behind the calendar used in the west according to which the revolution took place in November), they toppled the government and took control of Petrograd. In December the new Soviet government signed an armistice with Germany, although it was not until March 1918 that it accepted the extremely harsh peace terms of the Treaty of Brest–Litovsk.

2.6 1918

Figure 2.1: Map of the final German offensives in World War I (1918)

Source: Courtesy of the USMA, Department of History. https://www.usma.edu/history/SiteAssets/SitePages/World%20War%20I/WWOne18.jpg (accessed 23 May 2018)

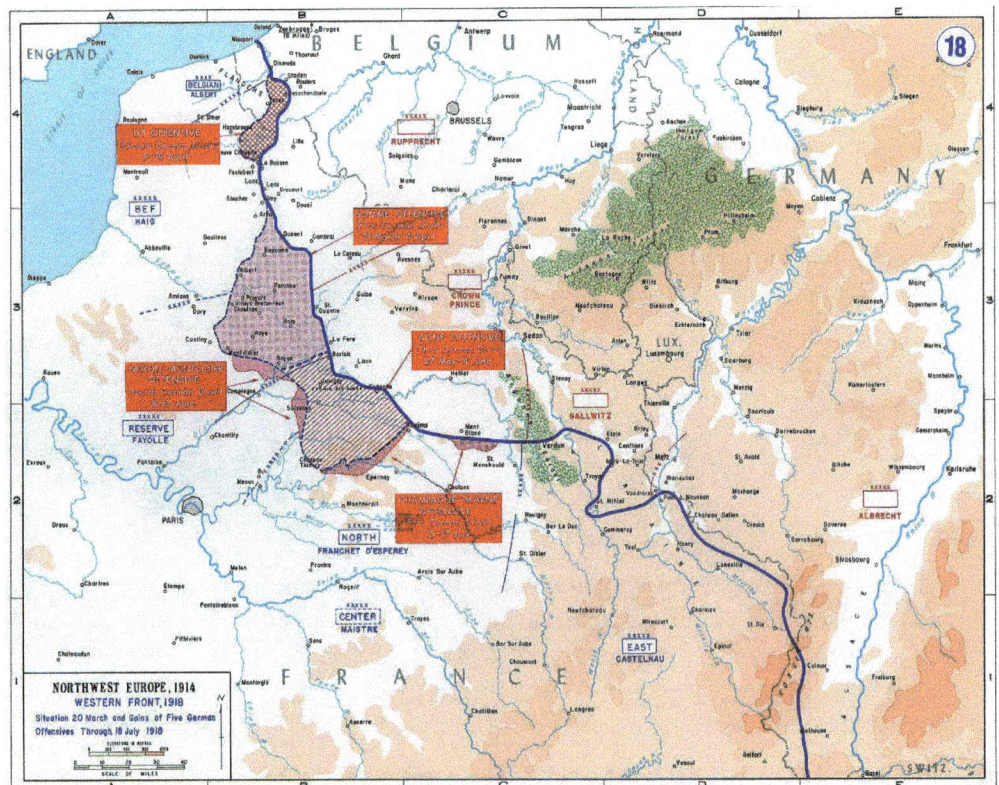

The year 1918 saw a dramatic return to a war of movement on the Western Front, with first the Germans achieving a major breakthrough in the spring, followed by a huge Allied counter-attack, beginning in the summer, which culminated in Germany seeking terms for surrender, which were signed on 11 November, ending the war.

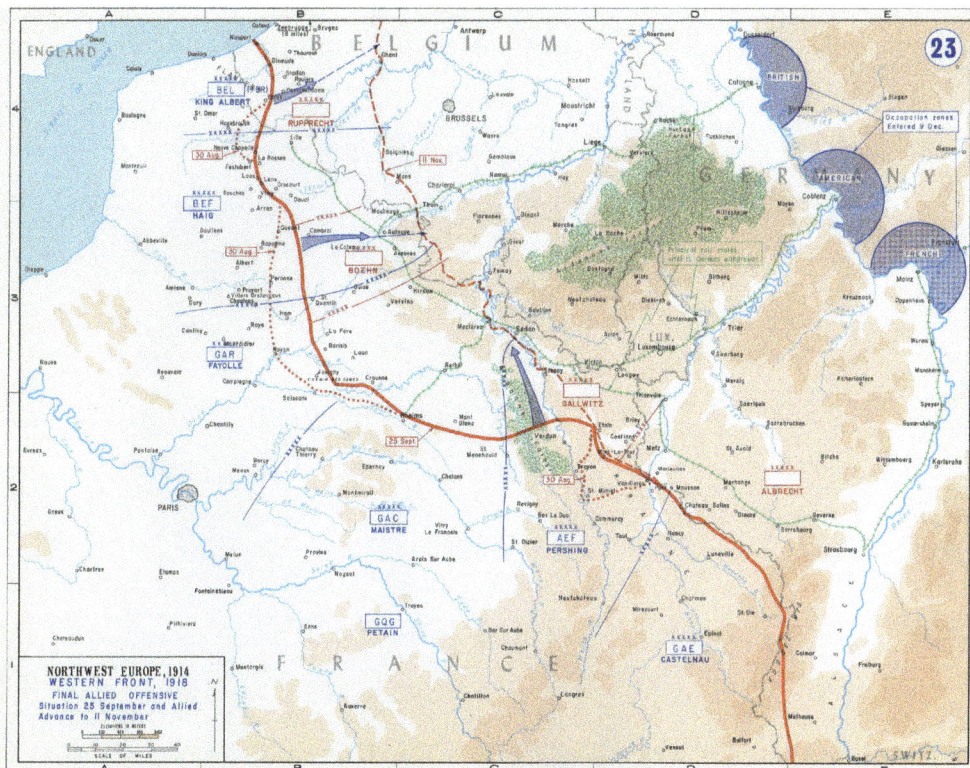

Figure 2.2: Map of the final Allied offensives in World War I (1918)

Source: Courtesy of the USMA, Department of History. https://www.usma.edu/history/SiteAssets/SitePages/World%20War%20I/WWOne23.pdf (accessed 23 May 2018)

⧗ TIMELINE

1918

MARCH ⌄	General Ludendorff launches Operation Michael, a massive German attack on a 100-kilometre front, which is strengthened by German troops moving from the Russian Front; however, many German troops have to remain in the eastern European territories Germany has now forced Russia to hand over. This is Ludendorff's last gamble as there are no German reserves left. Ludendorff had created special 'Storm Battalions' of troops trained to advance quickly. The attack takes place on the Somme, following a five-hour artillery barrage from 6,600 guns and the Germans, pushing forward 76 divisions, break through, inflicting 38,000 British casualties. Within five days some German units have advanced 65 km.
APRIL ⌄	A second huge surprise German attack occurs in the Ypres sector and the Germans make substantial gains: by July they are within 40 miles of Paris. Yet the Germans' success contains within it the seeds of failure because they lose large numbers of troops in making their breakthrough – 240,000 in Operation Michael by early April – and their forces are exhausted and over-stretched by their rapid advance. Furthermore, British and French forces retreat in an orderly fashion and, from late May, they are supported by US troops who now take the field. The above factors make the Germans very vulnerable to the Allied counter-offensive that started on 8 August at Amiens.
AUGUST ⌄	At Amiens, the British, French, and Americans take the Germans by surprise and a combination of improved communications (use of radio), extensive use of tanks and more sophisticated use of artillery to act as a cover for advancing infantry, result in a large-scale Allied breakthrough. By September the Allies have retaken all the ground they have lost in the German spring offensive and towards the end of the month had penetrated the Hindenburg Line.
6 OCTOBER ⌄	The German government asks the Allies for ceasefire terms.
9 NOVEMBER ⌄	The Kaiser flees to Holland and a republic is declared.
11 NOVEMBER	Germany's new socialist government, led by Friedrich Ebert, signs a ceasefire with the Allies, which brings the war to an end.

Figure 2.3: German General Headquarters: General Paul von Hindenburg, Kaiser Wilhelm II, General Erich Ludendorff

Source: Pixabay (CC0 1.0). https://pixabay.com/en/kaiser-wilhelm-ii-63116/ (accessed 12 April 2018)

> ## KEY ISSUES
>
> ### Why did Germany seek peace in 1918?
>
> 1. Ludendorff and Hindenburg were fully aware that, although the German Army could continue to fight on well into 1919, defeat was now unavoidable.
> 2. The failure of Ludendorff's spring offensives meant that Germany had few reserves left and the Allied counter-offensives of the summer and autumn seriously eroded German morale.
> 3. Fighting on two fronts for most of the war meant that Germany's military and economic resources were exhausted faster than the Allies'. Victory on the Eastern Front in March 1918 had come too late to save Germany from overall defeat.
> 4. From the summer of 1918, the Allies had shown much greater coordination in using artillery, tanks, and aircraft to support their infantry offensives and had also demonstrated greater cooperation between the French and British armies following Marshal Foch's appointment as supreme Allied commander-in-chief.
> 5. Before Germany surrendered, her allies had dropped out one by one. Austria-Hungary had already begun to implode by the autumn of 1918 as Czechs, Hungarians and Poles broke away as they sought to create their own independent states.
> 6. The Allies were able to call on far greater imperial resources than Germany. Over one million men from Canada, Australia, New Zealand and South Africa served in the British Army and 800,000 Indian troops were deployed in Mesopotamia (Iraq) alone. France raised 600,000 troops from its African colonies.
> 7. By Autumn 1918, 300,000 US troops were arriving each month in Europe. Germany's leaders estimated that, by 1919, they might face an army of up to five million Americans.
> 8. The USA's entry massively boosted the Allies economically. As Robert Wolfson and John Laver point out, in the first half of the war the industrial output of the Central Powers and the Triple Entente was roughly equal; both sets of powers produced about 350 million tons of coal and 20 million tons of steel. However, following the USA's entry into the war, the Allies' output climbed to over 840 million tons of coal and 58 million tons of steel, while the Central Powers' coal and steel production actually fell slightly (Wolfson and Laver, 1996, p. 217).
> 9. Discontent was mounting within Germany as strikes multiplied and socialists and communists staged risings in several northern German cities. Germany's soldiers, sailors, and civilians were angry to find out that Germany was on the verge of defeat after four years of hardship, extreme shortages and two million soldiers killed. At the start of November, there was a major mutiny by sailors based at Kiel. For a while it seemed as if Germany might follow Russia's recent example and undergo a violent revolution.

2.7 Technology and the Nature of Warfare in the First World War

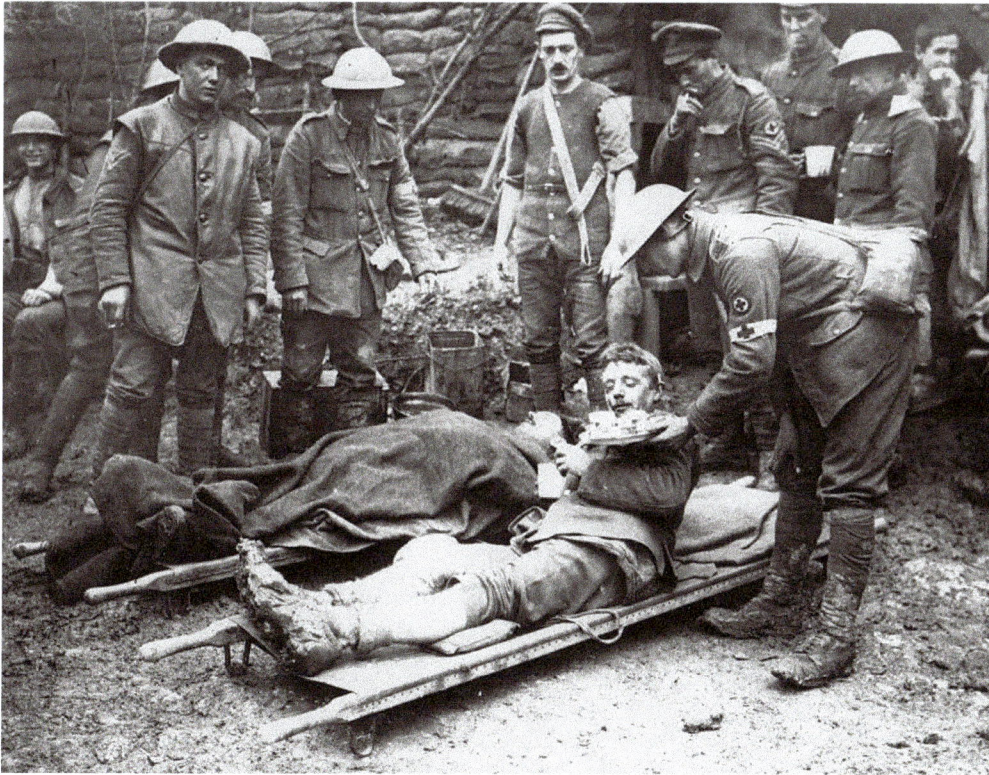

Figure 2.4: Two wounded soldiers lying on stretchers

Source: John Warwick Brooke (photographer), the National Library of Scotland (CC BY 4.0). http://digital.nls.uk/first-world-war-official-photographs/archive/74547382 (accessed 12 April 2018)

Industrialisation shaped the military technology deployed in the First World War, and this, in turn, determined the nature of the fighting. The **Boer War** (1899–1902) and the Russo-Japanese War (1904–5) had demonstrated the destructive capacity of modern weaponry but most military leaders in 1914 believed that the deployment of massed infantry, supported by artillery, could achieve a swift victory.

The last episode of general warfare in Europe prior to 1914 had been the Revolutionary and Napoleonic Wars ending in 1815. They had occurred at a time when industrialisation was only just under way in Europe. By 1914 Western Europe was highly industrialised, with Russia beginning to try to catch up rapidly from the 1890s. Along with changes in industry and agriculture, the nineteenth century also saw a huge growth in population.

Population growth, combined with every combatant nation, except Great Britain, employing conscription, meant unprecedentedly large armies could be mobilised in 1914. Europe's population numbered approximately 185 million in 1800 and then rose steeply to about 270 million by 1840 and in excess of 420 million by 1900. The size of armies had also grown enormously, with, for example, the German Army of 1914 being about ten times the size of the Prussian Army at the time of the Napoleonic Wars.

Industrialisation transformed the destructive power of weaponry, increasing the range, accuracy, and speed of fire and also the scale of production of weapons and ammunition. In Napoleon's day, infantry was equipped with muskets with an accurate range of just 60 metres; by 1914 magazine rifles had extended that distance to almost 1,500 metres and allowed infantry to fire at a rate seven times faster.

KEY TERMS

Boer War: War between Great Britain and the Boer republics in South Africa (1899–1902).

2.7.1 Technology and Stalemate on the Western Front

At the outbreak of the First World War, technological developments favoured the defender over the attacker. Both machine guns and artillery could be deployed much more effectively in defence than in attack, and, when barbed wire is added into the equation, the result was that, for much of the First World War, advancing infantry invariably suffered heavy casualties. This in turn explains why the Western Front came to be characterised by elaborate and extensive trench systems dug by both sides and usually consisting of three lines of trenches; the front lines hardly moved from late 1914 through to the spring of 1918 as the war in the West became stalemated.

The situation on the Eastern Front was very different and much more fluid; the much larger geographical scale of the Eastern Front allowed for greater manoeuvre and movement by the rival armies. Furthermore, German technological superiority over the Russian Army also contributed to rapid German advances deep into Russian territory.

2.7.2 Machine-guns

Until the later stages of the First World War, machine guns were much too heavy to be carried into attack and so, with a rate of fire of 600 rounds a minute and a range of 2,000–2,500 metres, they provided defenders with a massive advantage. In 1915 the British set up the Machine Gun Corps to coordinate deployment of machine guns across its armies, and, by 1918, they had 120,000 men serving in it. All of the combatant nations developed lighter machine guns as the war progressed, with the British manufacturing the Lewis Gun. By 1918 German assault troops were equipped with much lighter sub-machine guns (or 'machine pistols' as they were first described).

2.7.3 Artillery

Until 1918, artillery, the dominant weapon of the First World War, which accounted for 70% of total casualties, favoured the defending force. Artillery had been revolutionised in the 1870s by the development of field guns employing hydraulics where only the barrel moved rather than the whole gun allowing a much faster firing rate as guns did not need to be resighted after each shot; rates of fire rose from two rounds a minute (during the Franco-Prussian War of 1870–71) to eight rounds a minute. Until more sophisticated artillery techniques and tactics were developed in the second half of the First World War, artillery favoured the defence over an attacking force as it was insufficiently accurate to provide cover for advancing infantry, leaving it exposed to the deadly effects of the defending side's artillery.

All of the combatant countries (Germany rather less so) experienced serious shell shortages in the first year of the war as industry failed initially to keep up with the insatiable demand of the guns. In the Boer War, the British Army had expended 250,000 shells but, in the first six months of the First World War, British forces fired over one million. The French Army needed 100,000 shells a day but, in 1914, French industry was only producing 14,000 a day. Compounding this problem, as military planners had expected a war of movement, relatively little in the way of high-explosive shells, designed for destroying enemy fortifications, were available. Instead, the armies of 1914 were largely supplied with shrapnel shells designed to mow down infantry on the battlefield but of little value in taking out enemy strong points and defensive emplacements. 90% of British shells manufactured in 1914 were shrapnel.

In 1915 the combatant nations all took measures to increase massively their output of artillery and infantry ammunition, with Britain setting up the Ministry of Munitions in June. British shell production increased from 500,000 in 1914 to six million in 1915 and soared to almost 46 million in 1916.

Similarly, at the start of the war armies had mainly mobile field guns, designed to provide covering fire on a mobile battlefield, and relatively few heavy guns capable of firing high-explosive shells. Once the war of movement had given way to a static war of trenches on the Western Front, the need was for large numbers of heavy guns or howitzers. In 1914 France had just 300 heavy guns; by 1918 this had risen to 7,000.

Throughout 1915–17, infantry attacks were preceded by massive artillery bombardments, designed to destroy the barbed wire and trench defences of the enemy. However, these tactics invariably failed because:

- The artillery bombardment sacrificed the element of surprise
- The bombardment churned up the ground over which the attacking infantry had to advance and was at best only partially successful in clearing the barbed wire.

Field Marshal Haig was confident in launching the Battle of the Somme in July 1916 because he believed that the preliminary week-long bombardment of the German defences by 1.7 million shells would enable the British infantry to capture the German trenches with only light casualties. Instead, most of the Germans, sheltering in concrete bunkers up to 10 metres deep, survived the shelling and the British lost 57,000 men on the first day of their attack.

In 1917, at the Third Battle of Ypres, the British fired 4.3 million shells at the German forces east of the Ypres salient, but this destroyed the drainage system of the surrounding area and heavy rain turned it into a swamp, making the British advance up the Passchendaele Ridge painfully slow and very costly in lives.

🔑 KEY ISSUES

Why was the Western Front for much of the war characterised by trench warfare?

De Groot (2001) explains why the Western Front until 1918 was characterised by static trench warfare:

> Warfare is shaped by the interplay of firepower and mobility. When firepower is in the ascendancy, the war is static. When methods of movement allow the battlefield to be crossed with sufficient speed and protection, the war is mobile. In this war, mobility came in the form of primitive motor transport, the horse, or – the most common form – men simply walking. Movement was impeded by the boggy, shell-churned ground which made the battlefield inaccessible to trucks and motorcycles, and slowed the pace at which a fully equipped soldier could walk…The combatants, on the other hand, had access to a wide variety and virtually limitless supply of lethal firepower: artillery, rifles, mortars, machine guns, bombs and mines. In other words, firepower was dominant…There was little a soldier could do to advance against this firepower, therefore the natural response was to dig a hole. When millions of men dug holes the result was a trench system stretching from Switzerland to the English Channel. Because technology forced men into the trenches, but did not provide a way to get them out, the soldiers instead directed their energies to improving their trench systems by making them more impregnable.
>
> De Groot, 2001, pp. 29–30

2.7.4 Case Study: The Battle of Neuve Chapelle (March 1915)

The British attack at Neuve Chapelle illustrates the problems experienced by armies attempting to achieve a breakthrough on the Western Front in 1915–17. The British unleashed a short but very intensive artillery bombardment, and then the 60,000-strong infantry advanced on a narrow 8,000-metre front. Unusually, the British achieved almost total surprise and broke through the German front line. However, the Germans still held the flanks and were able to inflict heavy casualties on the British crowded into the narrow 1,500 metre gap in the front line. Two German machine guns killed approximately 1,000 British infantry in just two hours before British artillery took them out.

An even greater problem facing the British, and indeed attacking forces in general, related to communication. The telephone was a relatively efficient means of communicating between the front line and headquarters, but communications had to be relayed along the command chain: in the case of Neuve Chapelle via battalion, brigade, divisional, and corps headquarters (the latter being five miles back from the front), which took a very long time. Communication between senior commanders and troops who had advanced beyond their own front line was extremely difficult. Without radio, communication took the form of flag signals or runners: the first often obscured, the latter slow and vulnerable. At Neuve Chapelle, it took over nine hours from the point at which the British broke through for the order to continue the attack to be received by the troops who had occupied part of the German front line. This was shortly before darkness fell, and the next day when the attack was renewed the British could make no further progress in the face of hastily reinforced German defences.

Neuve Chapelle demonstrates that, even when advancing, infantry could penetrate the enemy's front line and this did prove possible quite frequently; invariably the defending side was able to move reserves up to plug any gap which opened up more quickly than the attacker could move its reserves forward. An attacking force that kept its reserves too far forward risked suffering heavy casualties from enemy artillery and would almost certainly sacrifice any element of surprise (Keegan, 1998, pp. 208–213).

De Groot analyses why the French Champagne offensive in September 1915 faltered after an initial advance of over 2 km:

> An immutable law of static war had once again been demonstrated. Any advance merely pushed enemy troops closer to their reinforcements, while lengthening the distance that the second wave of attackers had to travel in order to consolidate or extend the advance. The problems of capitalizing upon an initial success would plague armies for the entire war.

De Groot, pp. 37–38

2.7.5 Attrition

Commanders in the First World War, at first, expected a war of movement in which massed infantry and cavalry would make rapid advances. At the outbreak of war, the Germany Army comprised 87 infantry divisions and 11 cavalry divisions, while the French Army fielded 75 infantry and 10 cavalry divisions. However, cavalry, although proving valuable for reconnaissance in the opening months of the war, proved too vulnerable to the firepower of modern artillery and machine-guns. It should be noted that cavalry continued to be deployed to some effect on the Eastern Front where the greater distances meant that the war was less static than in the west.

Once the war of movement in France and Belgium gave way in late 1914 to a war of trenches, commanders on the Western Front sought to achieve major breakthroughs of the enemy trench systems, continuing to hope that they could deploy cavalry once that breakthrough had been made. However, the failure of any British and French offensive of 1915 to gain significant advances and, the resulting heavy casualties, caused them to accept that the war would be won by attrition.

KEY TERMS

Attrition: The strategy of wearing down an enemy by a series of offensives, causing the enemy to reach the point at which their resources and will to go on expired before their own did.

Perhaps the classic battle of attrition was Verdun in 1916 where Falkenhayn, the German commander-in-chief, aimed 'to bleed France white' by attacking Verdun, and, in the process, suck in and kill vast numbers of Frenchmen. To an extent, Falkenhayn achieved his aim as the French suffered over 500,000 casualties at Verdun; however, German casualties were not much less, at over 400,000.

The great British offensives of 1916–17 – the Somme and the Third Battle of Ypres – were represented by Field Marshal Haig as successful battles of attrition in which substantial damage was inflicted on the German Army. However, it seems that Haig originally intended to achieve quick breakthroughs in both cases and, only when they failed to materialise, did he then resign himself to a succession of attritional offensives. Moreover, the British Army suffered very similar casualties to the German Army in these battles, for example, on the Somme their losses were roughly 400,000, with the Germans suffering 500,000 casualties.

2.7.6 Technological and Tactical Developments during the First World War

Gas

The French used tear gas right from the start of the war but it was not until April 1915 that poison gas was first deployed, when the Germans discharged chlorine gas from cylinders, which blew towards the Allies during the Second Battle of Ypres. Perhaps 5,000 French and Algerian troops were killed after inhaling the gas, but Canadian troops plugged the gap in the front line.

The British Army first used poison gas at the Battle of Loos in October 1915. The German Army used phosgene gas in December 1915 and mustard gas in 1917. From July 1915 gas shells, fired by artillery, replaced cylinders as a more effective delivery system. Both sides quickly developed gas masks and equipped their soldiers with them. Although poison gas was widely feared by soldiers and was responsible for about one million casualties (inflicting terrible injuries, including blindness), relatively few soldiers died as a result of gas because gas mask design progressed quickly during the war.

Tanks

From 1914 Colonel Ernest Swinton was the driving force behind the tank's development. Swinton received support from Winston Churchill, first lord of the admiralty, who set up the Landships Committee in February 1915. The tank – whose codename during its development phase was intended to give the impression that it was a mobile water tank – was intended to restore mobility to the Western Front by providing a means of breaking through the barbed wire and taking out trench defences.

By 1916 a limited number of primitive tanks had been manufactured, but Swinton urged Field Marshal Haig not to deploy them until larger numbers were available so that they could be sent into action in massed formations. However, Haig by September 1916 was desperate for a breakthrough on the Somme and insisted on using the few tanks ready for action. The British Mark I tank, mounted on caterpillar tracks, was crewed by eight men and was equipped with either four Vickers machine guns or with six-pounder guns. Only 32 went into action on 15 September, and, although they terrified the Germans and enabled British troops to capture Flers, no strategic gains were made: too few were available to make a real impact, they were prone to mechanical breakdown, and they only had a top speed of 6 km per hour.

At Cambrai, in November 1917, 378 British tanks were sent into action, many of them carrying brushwood fascines for dropping into trenches so that the tanks could cross them. A 10-kilometre hole was punched into the German lines but lack of coordination with the infantry and organised German counter-attacks meant that the gap was soon plugged. Furthermore, the limitations of the tank were highlighted by the loss of 179 tanks on the first day of the battle.

The German government remained sceptical about the value of the tank and it was not until 1918 that the Germans deployed tanks and then only a tiny number (20). By contrast, the British and French developed tank technology considerably by the final year of the war and massed tank formations contributed to the success of the Allied counter-offensives of August–November 1918. However, it was not until after the First World War that improved tank design, making tanks much faster and less prone to mechanical failure, transformed the tank into a key weapon in land battles.

Artillery

In 1917 the British developed 'silent registering', which meant that targets could be registered for artillery bombardment without the need for range firing (test firing to establish accurately that the guns were locked on to the required target). Range firing had had the major disadvantage of forfeiting the element of surprise. By the time of the Allied counter-offensives of the summer and autumn of 1918, 'predicted shooting', aided by more precise and detailed maps resulting from aerial photography, helped ensure that artillery could be deployed more successfully to cover advancing infantry.

2.7.7 New Approaches to Trench Defences and Infantry Tactics

During the winter of 1916–17, German commanders altered their approach to their defences on the Western Front, adopting the idea of 'elastic defence in depth'.

- Fewer troops were stationed in the front zone of approximately 500–1000 m depth, with the main defensive forces holding up to three lines of trenches.
- Behind the trenches, up to a depth of 2000 m was a patchwork of camouflaged concrete pillboxes.
- Behind the main defensive zone special counter-attack units were ready waiting.

The Germans were able to wipe out entire battalions of French and British infantry who penetrated the front lines by isolating them within the main defensive zone, counter-attacking from the flanks. The development of these new tactics coincided with their withdrawal to the Hindenburg Line, a powerful network of defences consisting of three lines of double trenches. German front line defences were now characterised by a series of zig-zagging concrete pillboxes, equipped with machine guns and cannons, with interlocking fields of fire.

Until 1917 the standard approach to infantry tactics was a head-on attack by extended lines of infantry following on an extensive artillery barrage. New infantry tactics were devised first by the Germans in 1917.

- This involved specially trained storm troopers in small units, moving at speed, infiltrating enemy lines and avoiding enemy strong points.
- The infantry advance was to be preceded by a much shorter but very intense artillery bombardment. The artillery targeted the enemy's rear positions, headquarters and artillery, before focusing on the enemy's forward positions shortly before the attack.

These tactics were first used by the Germans on the Eastern Front in September 1917 and constituted a major reason for the initial success of Ludendorff's spring offensives in 1918. The German Army reduced the number of soldiers per division while increasing their firepower to include 50 trench mortars and 350 machine guns per division.

Similarly, by 1918 the Allies had developed new tactics and used tanks, air craft, artillery and infantry in a much more coordinated way than previously. The 8 August 1918 saw the start of the Battle of Amiens, the first in a series of Allied offensives which culminated in Germany's surrender on 11 November. The British were able to advance almost 13 km on the first day thanks to the combination of artillery using silent registration, air attacks and 530 tanks. The development of radio communication, by then, made for more coordinated offensives.

Figure 2.5: British Mark I Male tank, the Somme, 25 September 1916

Source: Ernest Brooks (photographer), the National Library of Scotland (CC BY 4.0). https://digital.nls.uk/first-world-war-official-photographs/archive/74546688 (accessed 12 April 2018)

2.7.8 The War in the Air

It was only eleven years before the outbreak of the war that the Wright brothers had made the first flight. In August 1914 very few military aircraft were in service. Aircraft were not to play a decisive role in affecting the course or outcome of the First World War but they did develop very rapidly in terms of numbers, technology, and capability. In 1914 the few planes possessed by the combatant nations were very fragile and prone to mechanical failure.

2.7.9 Aerial Reconnaissance

Throughout the war reconnaissance was the most important role for aircraft and airships, as they quickly took over the task traditionally carried out by cavalry. As early as September 1914, it was the Royal Flying Corps that spotted the German First Army changing its route around Paris that led the Allies to launch the successful counter-attack on the Marne. Photographic reconnaissance enabled military cartographers to produce extremely precise maps of enemy trench systems and defences, which were essential for effective artillery bombardments. Air-to-ground communications improved through the course of the war and meant that aircraft could guide artillery to fire accurately on to their targets.

2.7.10 Design Developments

Both sides saw the importance of denying aerial intelligence to their enemy but initially aircrew were only issued with revolvers and rifles, and it was impractical to shoot down enemy aircraft. However, July 1915 marked the advent of forward-firing machine guns, developed first by Anthony Fokker for the Germans – he designed a machine-gun mechanism that, by means of an interrupter, ensured that the bullets fired would not hit the plane's propeller blade. This gave rise to the fighter plane and the air 'aces' – the pilots who gained fame through the number of 'kills' they registered in dogfights with enemy aircraft. The most successful pilots became household names, feted in the press and newsreels of the time – Major Edward 'Mick' Mannock of Great Britain with 73 kills, Captain René Fonck of France with 75 and, most celebrated of all, Manfred von Richthofen, the 'Red Baron', with 80 kills for Germany.

The balance of the air war oscillated between Germany and the Allies, very largely as the result of changes in technology as faster and more manoeuvrable planes were developed.

- In 1915 German pilots, with their Fokker planes, held the advantage.
- In 1916 the introduction of the French Nieuport XVII and the British DH2 gave Allied pilots the edge over their German counterparts.
- The Germans regained their dominance with a vengeance in late 1916 when they introduced the twin-gunned Albatros fighters. By April 1917, known as 'Bloody April', heavy losses were being inflicted on Britain's Royal Flying Corps.
- However, from that point onwards the Allies regained the initiative with new aircraft including the Sopwith Triplane and the Sopwith Camel. The Sopwith Camel achieved 2,880 kills, the most by any type of Allied fighter.
- The Germans did introduce their best fighter of the war, the Fokker DVII, in April 1918; but in 1918 the Allies enjoyed a marked superiority in numbers of planes, aided by the 740 US aircraft on the Western Front by the summer of that year.

2.7.11 Strategic Bombing

As early as September 1914, the Royal Naval Air Service (RNAS), carried out strategic bombing, attacking Zeppelin (airship) hangers in Dusseldorf. However, accurate bombing was only made possible in 1915 with the development of bomb-sights and, although bomb payloads did increase significantly in the last three years of the war, the size and quantity of bombs carried by planes were insufficient to make a real impression on either enemy defences or civilian targets.

Nonetheless, psychological air raids on towns and cities had a profound and unsettling effect on civilians. In the case of Great Britain, civilians for the first time learnt that they were not safe in their island fortress. Initially the Germans used, from January 1915, huge 650 feet long airships, Zeppelins, to drop bombs on London and other parts of South East England. It took until 1916 for Britain to develop effective anti-aircraft guns, searchlights and barrage balloons. Zeppelin raids killed 556 British civilians altogether.

From 1917 the Germans continued strategic bombing with Gotha aeroplanes, rather than with Zeppelins, which proved highly vulnerable to the anti-aircraft measures referred to above. In 1917–18, in total 835 British civilians died as a result of such raids. The British government responded in 1918 by developing their own strategic bomber, the Handley Page, which had a range of almost 2,000 km and a payload of 900 kg.

2.7.12 Tactical Bombing

Tactical bombing developed during the First World War but was only employed to a limited extent.

In the Third Battle of Ypres, in the autumn of 1917, the RFC flew low-level missions aimed at weakening German defences. Air power contributed significantly to British victory against Turkey in the Middle East in 1917, with the bombers of Britain's Palestine Brigade inflicting heavy casualties on the Turkish Seventh and Eighth Armies. During the Allied offensives of August–November 1918, the RAF was deployed in a variety of ways to assist infantry and artillery.

KEY TERMS

Strategic bombing: The strategy of wearing down an enemy by sustained bombing raids, causing the enemy to reach the point at which their resources and will to go on expires. Strategic bombing targets industrial and civilian centres.

Tactical bombing: The use of aircraft to support ground troops by attacking enemy personnel, using machine guns and bombs.

2.7.13 Aircraft's Role in the War at Sea

One area where aircraft played an increasingly valuable role was the war at sea, with the Germans using Zeppelins as a scouting force from the outset of the war. Great Britain had set up the Royal Naval Air Service in July 1914 and used it to provide valuable intelligence about the whereabouts of German surface ships and U-boats.

Rapid technological progress was made: in 1917 a Sopwith Pup made the first successful landing on an aircraft carrier and the first successful take off from a plane from a ship also took place. Sea planes were also developed: for example, the Sopwith Baby could fire rockets at balloons and drop explosive darts on U-boats or Zeppelins flying at low altitude.

Aircraft equipped with torpedoes were also used by the British to counter the U-boat menace. When the British introduced the convoy system in 1917 to protect merchant ships, air cover proved extremely valuable; in convoys accompanied by planes not a single ship was sunk.

The air war's growing importance was reflected by Britain's establishment in April 1918 of the Royal Air Force (RAF) as an independent air force (separate from the navy and army). By the war's end, the RAF had almost 300,000 personnel. More than half of Britain's 22,000 pilots were injured or killed during the war. There were 8,000 aircraft on all sides on the Western Front in 1918.

2.7.14 The War at Sea

Ironically, given that the Anglo-German naval race had played an important part in generating the tension that was to lead to the First World War, there was to be only one major set-piece battle between the battle fleets of Great Britain and Germany. Both countries were all too aware that a decisive defeat in battle could allow its enemy to achieve control of the seas and, in turn, control of supplies. At the outbreak of war, the British Navy was the most powerful in the world, with 22 Dreadnoughts to Germany's 15, 40 other battleships to Germany's 22, and 130 cruisers to Germany's 45 (De Groot, p. 75).

Although both countries adopted a cautious approach, their strategies differed: Britain was content to impose a long-distance blockade on Germany while the German Navy sought to pick off small parts of their British counterpart, after luring them out to sea, eventually reducing the Royal Navy's strength to a point where the German High Seas Fleet could consider a full-scale battle.

There were a series of small-scale naval engagements in 1914–15 in which the Germans achieved some success, including the *Goeben* and *Breslau* managing to elude a British squadron in the Mediterranean and get to Constantinople. In December 1914 German ships shelled the east coast of England, killing over 100 civilians, leading to the sinking of the *Blucher* by the British at Dogger Bank in January 1915. Two months earlier, Vice-Admiral von Spee's East Asian Squadron sank two British cruisers at Cape Coronel off the coast of Chile. However, von Spee's squadron was destroyed by the British at the Battle of the Falkland Islands in December, and by July 1915 all of Germany's squadrons at sea were eliminated and the German High Seas Fleet remained hemmed in its home ports until the end of May 1916.

2.7.15 The British Naval Blockade

Early in the war the British had captured German naval codes and this proved a huge advantage to the British in monitoring German naval operations. Britain continued to apply a long-distance blockade with the Grand Fleet based at Scapa Flow in the Orkneys and Rosyth in the Firth of Forth, about 800 km from Germany's harbours. Patrols by cruisers and armed merchant ships intercepted ships passing between Iceland and Scotland, seizing 'contraband' supplies destined for Germany. The alternative strategy of a short-range blockade might have prevented the Germans from accessing the Baltic, Belgian, and Dutch ports but would have increased the likelihood of serious naval losses by Britain.

2.7.16 The Battle of Jutland (1916)

Figure 2.6: Map showing the movements of the British and German fleets during the Battle of Jutland (1916)

Source: Courtesy of the USMA, Department of History. https://www.usma.edu/history/ SiteAssets/SitePages/World%20 War%20I/WWOne45.jpg (accessed 23 May 2018)

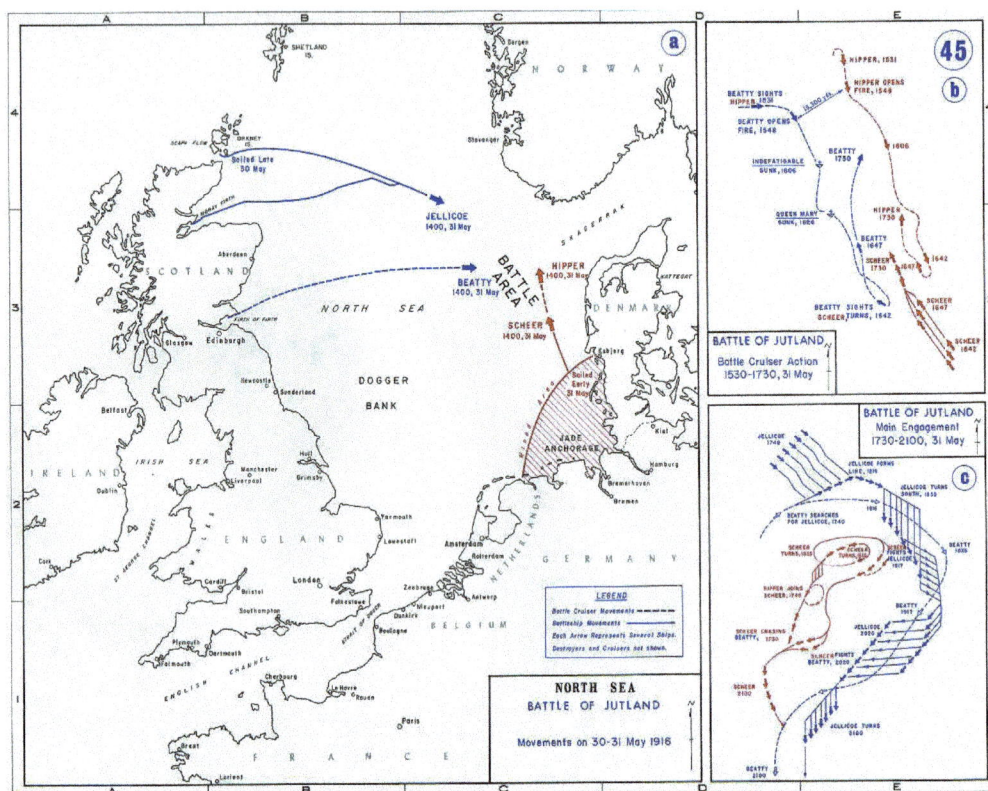

The one large-scale naval battle of the war took place at Jutland in the North Sea on 31 May–1 June 1916: it was fought over 36 hours and involved 259 ships. Admiral Hipper led out Germany's battle cruisers in an attempt to lure out the British Navy into the path of Germany's battleships. British radio surveillance meant that Admiral Jellicoe was aware of what the Germans were planning, and he sent Admiral Beatty, commanding Britain's battle cruisers, in pursuit. The fleets began exchanging fire at just before 4.00 pm on 31 May. Jellicoe's Dreadnoughts joined the battle after Beatty had engaged Hipper's force and twice **crossed Scheer's 'T'**, positioning his fleet across the German route home. However, poor communications and nightfall prevented the British from attempting to achieve a decisive result and the German High Seas Fleet was able to withdraw and return to port safely.

The British, whose armour-plating and gunnery proved inferior to the Germans', lost 14 ships and over 6,000 men while the Germans lost 11 ships and around 2,500 men. Although British losses in ships and men were higher than Germany's, strategically the battle was a victory for Britain as its blockade remained intact and the German fleet did not attempt to leave port for the remainder of the war.

🔑 **KEY TERMS**

Crossing the T: Naval tactic in which a line of warships crosses in front of a line of enemy ships, so that they can open fire with all their guns, while the enemy ships can only use their forward guns.

2.7.17 The Impact of the British Naval Blockade

The economic blockade on Germany was of great importance as the war wore on. Germany increasingly suffered severe shortages of raw materials and food. In turn, this adversely affected supplies of weapons and ammunition for her armed forces and civilian morale on the Home Front. Up to an estimated 750,000 German civilians died in 1914–18 because of the effects of malnutrition, resulting from food shortages. By contrast, Britain was able to use its control of the seas to transport troops and supplies from both the British Isles and its empire to France and to keep Britain fed and its war industries supplied with chemicals and other vital raw materials. However, Britain's lifeline was seriously threatened in 1917, not by Germany's surface fleet, but by its submarines (U-boats).

2.7.18 Submarine Warfare

At the start of the war Germany possessed 21 U-boats for use in the North Sea to attack ships supplying Britain and France. In May 1915 a German U-boat off the coast of Ireland sank a passenger liner, the *Lusitania*, travelling from the USA. Nearly 1,200 civilians were drowned, including over 100 Americans, and the ensuing US protest led the German government to suspend its unrestricted U-boat attacks. U-boat attacks continued but only after ships were warned.

By January 1917 Germany had built a fleet of 110 U-boats and its military commanders were confident that unrestricted submarine warfare could starve Britain into submission. Such a campaign was announced on 1 February, with Germany's leaders fully aware that this would almost inevitably provoke the USA's entry into the war as its merchant ships, which were supplying Britain and France, would be targeted. The USA duly declared war on Germany in April, but the German government assumed that it could win the war before the USA was able to get significant numbers of troops into Europe. Certainly, the Germans in the spring–summer of 1917 inflicted huge losses on Allied and neutral merchant shipping, bringing Britain's food stocks down to dangerously low levels. In February 1917 German U-boats sank almost 550,000 tonnes of shipping, rising to 894,000 tonnes in August of that year.

2.7.19 Britain's Response to the U-boat Threat

Faced by the prospect of being unable to sustain its war effort because of the shortages in supplies, Britain was obliged, alongside food rationing, to take counter measures to deal with the U-boat menace.

- Decoy or 'Q' ships were deployed along with **depth charges**, hydrophones (for detecting U-boats) and aircraft were equipped with torpedoes.
- Moreover, the British prime minister (David Lloyd George) insisted, against the objections of the Admiralty, on the introduction of the convoy system in May 1917, with flotillas of merchant ships being escorted across the Atlantic, Mediterranean, and North Sea by destroyers. Whereas in April 1917, 25% of merchant shipping was sunk by U-boats, only 1% of shipping in convoys was sunk.

By the end of the war, German U-boats had sunk over 6,000 Entente and neutral ships totalling 11.9 million tonnes, but in the process 178 U-boats had been lost, with almost 30% of Germany's submariners ending up as casualties.

KEY TERMS

Depth charge: An anti-submarine weapon which consisted of a canister filled with explosives that was dropped off the stern of a ship. It would explode at a predetermined depth.

2.8 Total War and the Home Front

'Total war' was a phrase first coined by General Ludendorff in 1918; it means the mobilisation of all the resources of a country for warfare. The harnessing of a nation's economy to the demands of 'total war' led combatant governments to view the enemy population as a whole as a legitimate target.

Historians regard the First World War as the first example of total warfare as it was the first occasion since Europe had underwent industrialisation that a general European war had broken out. As the war developed into a prolonged conflict (a war of attrition), the demands for ammunition and weaponry – as well as clothing, food and transport – to supply the sinews of war reached staggering levels.

A few statistics will serve to illustrate the insatiable demands on industry and agriculture.
- In September 1918 the British Army was firing 2.2 million shells every week.
- Over the course of the war, the British shipped to continental Europe over 33 million people, 2.5 million horses, 500,000 vehicles, and 49 million tons of equipment and supplies.
- France's factories turned out 35,000 aircraft, 5,000 tanks, 350,000 telephones, and two million km of cable.

Winston Churchill became the British minister of munitions in 1917 and the following description by him of the enormous power of his ministry conveys the scale of government economic control that developed during the war to a lesser or greater degree in all the combatant nations:

> Nearly all the mines and workshops of Britain were in our hands. We controlled and were actually managing all the greatest industries. We regulated the supply of all their raw materials. We organised the whole distribution of their finished products. Nearly five million persons were directly under our orders, and we were interwoven on every side with every sphere of the national economic life.

Terraine, p. 133

In short, governments in all combatant countries had to devote much of their attention to organising their home fronts as they would prove vital to sustaining the fighting on the various military fronts.

2.8.1 Case Study 1: The Home Front in Great Britain

Economic mobilisation and rationing
- In July 1915 David Lloyd George was appointed to run the new Ministry of Munitions to solve the shell shortages affecting Britain's armed forces. Later, as prime minister from December 1916, Lloyd George set up a Ministry of Labour and a Ministry of Food to coordinate war production and food supplies.
- The Munitions of War Act (1915) empowered the government to regulate workers by banning strikes and ending restrictive working practices in some industries.
- Voluntary rationing was encouraged by the British government in 1917 following Germany's unrestricted U-boat attacks that sank one in four British merchant ships in the spring and summer.
- In January 1918 sugar rationing was introduced; in April this was extended to meat, butter, and cheese.
- During the war, to boost food production, the government took control of over 2.5 million acres of unused land.

Financing the war
The government spent a total of £9,593 billion on the war. To finance this:
- It borrowed heavily both at home and from the USA.

- It increased the amount of paper currency massively: in 1914 the total value of notes in circulation was just under £34 million; by 1915 this had risen to over £89 million and continued to soar for the remainder of the war.
- Taxes rose steeply. Income tax was increased from one shilling in the pound to six shillings in the pound between 1914 and 1918.

KEY INFORMATION

240 pence = 1 pound
12 pence = 1 shilling
20 shilling = 1 pound

KEY ISSUES

How did the war affect women?

- Gradually women replaced male factory workers who had left to fight. However, the trade unions were not cooperative, fearful that employers would prefer to recruit women whom they could pay cheaper wages to. By 1915 Britain faced serious shell shortages so the government set up munitions factories and employed women in them; in 1915 Lloyd George got the trade unions to agree that women could take over just for the duration of the war, until the men returned from the fighting.
- Because of the insatiable demands of the armed forces for weapons and ammunition, many more women were employed in industry, especially in munitions factories: for example, by 1918 there were 700,000 in metal and chemical industries compared to only 200,000 in 1914, while the number of women employed in munitions factories rose from 210,000 in 1914 to 950,000 by 1918.
- Many women joined a variety of voluntary organisations to support the war effort: for example, the Women's Land Army, which was established to replace male farm workers and to increase food production because of food shortages. The Women's Police Volunteers were set up in 1914.
- The Voluntary Aid Detachment (VAD) recruited 8,000 nurses for the Western Front.
- The Women's Auxiliary Army Corps (WAACs) enlisted 40,000 women who took on army clerical and other support work as telephone operators, drivers, cooks, and storekeepers.

2.8.2 The Defence of the Realm Act (DORA): August 1914

This gave the British government wide powers to censor newspapers and ration food. It was extended as the war progressed. The government made regular use of propaganda, such as the film *The Battle of the Somme*, which an estimated 20 million Britons watched, to mobilise support for the war. There was a variety of government campaigns, which included trying to get civilians to do voluntary work and to buy less food.

- In 1915 public house opening hours were reduced and beer was made weaker to prevent production being affected by absenteeism due to excessive drinking.
- British Summer Time (involving the changing of the clocks by one hour) was introduced to maximise daylight hours for war production.

2.8.3 Recruitment

5.7 million men served in the British Army: 22% of the adult male population. Unique among the major combatants, Britain relied on voluntary recruitment until 1916. Recruitment campaigns were successfully organised by Lord Kitchener, secretary of state for war. Britain's army was transformed from a small standing professional force of about 200,000 men to a massive establishment of 2.5 million, as volunteers flooded in to form Britain's 'New Armies'; many of them were composed of 'pals battalions' (that is, units made up of men from the same factories or villages).

In 1916 the Military Service Act signaled a major change for Britain as **conscription** was introduced, first for single men (January), then married men (May) aged 18–41. Over two million men were conscripted. There were certain reserved occupations, such as coal mining, where men engaged in work vital for the war effort were exempt from compulsory military service.

Some men refused to join the army on grounds of principle, often because of their religious beliefs. In total, there were 16,000 **conscientious objectors**, or 'conshies' as they became known. The government set up work camps for them, while some acted as stretcher-bearers at the front. About 1,500 refused alternative service and were imprisoned.

2.8.4 Civilians under Fire

The First World War saw British civilians under direct attack. Civilians were no longer safe in Britain's island fortress. The German Navy shelled the coast of North East England in December 1914, resulting in over 100 civilians being killed.

British civilians also came under attack from the air, initially in the shape of Zeppelin raids from 1915 and later by large Gotha bombers. In total about 1,400 civilians died.

Because the economic capacity of the combatant nations proved increasingly important to their ability to sustain their war efforts, both sides tried to prevent overseas supplies from getting to their enemies. We have already seen that this became a central feature of the war at sea. In February 1917 the Germans launched unrestricted submarine warfare in an attempt to starve Britain into submission. Many British merchant seamen were drowned as a result, and, by the early summer of 1917, British food stocks were running seriously low but the U-boat menace lessened because of Britain's use of the convoy system and of Q-ships (armed ships disguised as merchant ships).

2.8.5 Case Study 2: The Home Front in Germany

Government economic control

Although the German government did set up the Raw Materials Department in August 1914, with the aim of enabling it to allocate raw materials to where the need was greatest, Germany proved much slower to adopt a significant degree of centralisation and state control in its economy compared to Great Britain and France; controls in Germany were also never as far reaching as in Britain and France.

It was not until the Hindenburg Programme of August 1916 that the German government really tried to get to grips with full economic mobilisation. This coincided with the military, particularly General Hindenburg and General Ludendorff, exerting growing control over the country. Some historians have written about a virtual 'military dictatorship' in Germany in the second half of the war. The situation in Britain and France was very different with Lloyd George and George Clemenceau retaining civilian control over the military.

The Hindenburg Programme laid down very ambitious production targets, including tripling machine gun and artillery production by May 1917, but the targets were not achieved. Under the Hindenburg Programme, non-essential industries were shut down.

The Auxiliary Labour Law of December 1916 obliged all men aged 17–60 to work, with the government given the power to determine which industries they would work in.

As in Britain, more women joined Germany's workforce. During the war, the number of female workers increased by 46%.

Financing the war

Germany, like all the combatant nations, raised the majority of the huge sums it spent on the war by increasing the amount of paper currency in circulation (by 1,141%) and

---

KEY TERMS

Conscription: Compulsory military service.

Conscientious objectors: People who refuse to do military service because they oppose war and fighting on moral or religious grounds.

by borrowing: for example, by issuing **war bonds** which civilians were encouraged to buy and which could be redeemed at the end of the war. Unlike Britain and France, Germany was unable to borrow money from the USA. One consequence was inflation, which proved much higher in Germany than in Britain and France.

The weakness of the Home Front in Germany

Germany and its allies proved less able to sustain the war economically than Britain, France, and the USA; this was one of the key factors affecting the eventual outcome of the conflict. The Allies were able to call on larger populations, with the result that they mobilised about 40 million soldiers in total compared to the Central Powers' 25 million, and greater industrial resources. The entry of the USA was critical in this respect as it transformed the economic balance of power between the Central Powers and the Entente. In 1918 the Allies' combined production in terms of coal, steel, and iron was nearly three times that of the Central Powers.

The relative weakness of the German Home Front is also explained by the impact of the British Naval Blockade, which resulted in increasing shortages and frequent food riots from 1916. An estimated 750,000 German civilians died as a result, succumbing to fatal diseases because they were weakened by malnutrition.

The naval blockade and the calling up of millions of men for the armed forces also meant that in the second half of the war industrial production actually declined in Germany. The productivity of German workers fell as a consequence of working long hours and food shortages, while factories faced fuel shortages. Similarly, agricultural production fell because a higher proportion of farm workers were conscripted in Germany than in France and Britain; both wheat and potato harvests in 1918 were only half of the average harvests for 1912–13. Rationing was introduced in 1915 and ersatz (substitute) foodstuffs and goods were developed such as bread made from potatoes.

As economic conditions worsened in Germany, there was growing unrest, as strikes increased, just as was the case in Britain and France. In January 1918 more than a million men in Germany went on strike and 'soviets' or councils chosen by workers and soldiers were set up to articulate the workers' grievances, which not only included the food shortages but also political demands, such as an end to the war and a new, more democratic government for Germany. However, it is important to note that, unlike in Russia, the Home Front in Germany did not collapse until after its leaders had already concluded that they could not win the war and had to look for peace terms from the Allies. Nonetheless, increasing demonstrations and strikes did contribute to Kaiser Wilhelm II's decision to abdicate in November 1918, as Germany seemed to be heading towards revolution.

Figure 2.7: Barricade during the Spartacus Rising. in Berlin in January 1919, when German Communists unsuccessfully tried to stage a revolution.

Source: *Berliner Illustrirte Zeitung*, via Wikimedia Commons (file uploaded by Ichwarsnur). https://commons.wikimedia.org/wiki/File:Spartakusaufstand_Barrikaden.jpg (accessed 12 April 2018)

KEY TERMS

War bonds: Government debt certificates, guaranteeing repayment with interest by the government at the end of the war.

3. THE EFFECTS OF THE FIRST WORLD WAR

Overview

This chapter addresses the effects of the First World War, both on individual countries' domestic history and internationally. I have selected three major combatants – Germany, Britain, and Italy – and examined the political, social, and economic impact of the war on them. In Chapter 2 I have also provided some detailed analysis of the impact of the war on Russia. With regards to the international effects of the First World War, I have adopted a thematic approach, analysing the economic and financial impact, the geopolitical impact (on the map of Europe and other regions of the world, following the peace settlement of 1919–20, and on the international balance of power) and the longer term question of whether the First World War can be seen to have made the Second World War inevitable/very likely: this question is one that has continued to divide historians, and I have considered the arguments for and against the proposition that the First World War made the Second World War inevitable or very likely.

3.1 Domestic Effects of the First World War

The war had profound effects on all of the combatant countries. First, we will briefly look at the war's impact on Germany and then, in greater detail, at the major consequences of the war on Britain and Italy.

Woodrow Wilson had declared that the First World War would be 'the war to make the world safe for democracy'; however, instead it helped give rise to a communist dictatorship in Russia and created the conditions which destabilised democracy in both Germany and Italy, giving rise to right-wing dictatorships. Yet democracy survived intact in France, Britain, and the USA, suggesting that other economic, social, and political conditions were present in Russia, Germany, and Italy – the First World War did not create them from nowhere but it did worsen them.

3.1.1 Germany

The war and subsequent peace settlement destabilised Germany politically and economically. The war, as indicated above, had caused serious inflation and shortages of food and goods. This, in turn, caused growing political unrest and contributed to Kaiser Wilhelm II's decision to abdicate in November 1918. Germany became a republic and experienced a succession of political and economic crises. The new democratic system did not enjoy stable political conditions until the mid-1920s as the government faced extremists on both the left (**Communists**) and the right (**Nationalists**) who sought to overthrow it. Many on the right blamed the democratic politicians who came to power in November 1918 for betraying the German Army, claiming it could have fought on but for the new government which signed the armistice. In addition to this 'stab-in-the-back legend', the Nationalists blamed the democratic politicians for signing the humiliating Treaty of Versailles in June 1919.

Economically, Germany suffered inflation, culminating in the disastrous hyper-inflation crisis of 1923. This was linked to the First World War because the German government printed more and more paper money to try to cover its debts from the war and had to contend with the French and Belgians occupying the Ruhr in 1923 after Germany stopped paying **reparations** imposed by the Treaty of Versailles. Germany was also weakened by the loss of important industrial areas such as part of Upper Silesia to Poland and the Saar, which was administered by the newly formed League of Nations until 1935, as a consequence of the Versailles Treaty.

The **Weimar Republic's** association with the hated Treaty of Versailles and its difficult first few years arguably made the survival of democracy in Germany less likely, but this did not make Hitler's rise to power inevitable. The latter was only made possible by the devastating impact of the Wall Street Crash (1929), in which the American Stock Market crashed, resulting in the withdrawal of American loans to Germany, and the **Great Depression** on Germany.

🔑 **KEY TERMS**

Communists: Political groups aiming to abolish private property as the result of a revolution. In Germany, the Communists sought to copy the success of Lenin's Bolsheviks who seized control in Russia in 1917.

Nationalists: Political groups who seek to make their country as strong as possible and who prioritise putting their countries' interests ahead of those of other countries. In the case of German nationalists, they also stood for the union of all German-speakers within a single German state.

Reparations: Germany was obliged by the Treaty of Versailles to pay £6,600 million in financial compensation to France, Britain, Italy and Belgium for damages inflicted during the First World War.

Weimar Republic: Germany between 1918 and 1933 is known as the Weimar Republic because it was in the town of Weimar that the constitution for the republic that was established in 1918, after the Kaiser abdicated, was drawn up.

Great Depression: The disastrous economic downturn that affected the USA and most industrialised economies in the early to mid-1930s, triggered by the Wall Street Crash.

3.1.2 Great Britain

In terms of the human cost, Britain lost 745,000 military personnel killed in the war. About 1.5 million soldiers were permanently injured.

Britain's financial and commercial strength were both significantly undermined by the First World War, and this undoubtedly played a part in reducing Britain's influence as a world power.

Financial weakness also explains Britain's rapid demobilisation of its armed forces after the war. Britain reduced its defence spending from £604 million (1919) to just £111 million three years later, and by the end of the 1920s, Britain's armed forces numbered only 180,000 men. At the Washington Naval Conference (1921–22), Britain accepted naval parity (equal numbers of warships) with the USA and agreed to build no new warships for 10 years. In terms of airpower, Britain had the world's largest air force in 1919, with 22,000 planes; within three years Britain's air force had been reduced to just 10% of the size of France's.

Britain's financial weakness and rapid postwar demobilisation, in turn, partly explain Britain's determination to avoid military commitments to other countries in the 1920s and 1930s and helped shape the British government's policy of appeasing Hitler and Mussolini in the 1930s, making concessions to avoid war.

State controls over the economy, introduced during the First World War, were ended when the war ended.

Welfare reforms, such as accident insurance for some workers and old age pensions, had been initiated before the First World War, starting in 1905. The war saw a continuation of this trend, for example: the introduction of free milk for infants and free school meals, and the acceleration of welfare reform after 1918, such as the Pension Act (1925), extended the provision of old age pensions. Between 1914 and 1933, the British government's spending on welfare as a percentage of **GNP** increased from 5.5% to 13%. So, welfare reform is a good example of where the war did not create a new trend but instead accelerated an existing one. The British government increased welfare spending partly in an attempt to ease the strains imposed on the civilian population by the transition from war to peacetime economy and in recognition of the hardships endured by its citizens during the war, whether on the battlefield or the home front.

The 1918 general election saw slogans such as 'homes fit for heroes', which created a widespread expectation that there would be a range of social reforms, including new housing, introduced at the end of the war. This indeed did happen and reforms included:

- The Education Act of 1918, which raised the school leaving age to 14
- The Ministry of Health, established in 1919
- The Housing Act of 1919, which mandated local authorities to construct new houses: 200,000 were built by 1922
- The Unemployment Insurance Act of 1920, which extended the terms of the 1911 Act so that most categories of workers earning less than £250 p.a. could claim unemployment benefit for up to 15 weeks a year.

Britain, along with other combatant countries, suffered from economic dislocation at the end of the war; by 1921 unemployment had reached 23% of the adult population. Throughout the years 1919–39 unemployment rarely fell below 10% and the period saw a

---

KEY TERMS

GNP: An abbreviation for Gross National Product. The total value of goods and services produced by a country.

decline in Britain's more traditional heavy industries like coal mining and shipbuilding, as Britain struggled to cope with greater competition from countries such as Germany and Poland. Again, this trend was evident before 1914, so the war acted as an accelerant. As mentioned earlier, British exporters lost markets overseas during the war to the USA and Japan, and these were to a large extent not regained after peace returned in 1918.

The war had led to major changes in the role and status of women in Britain as the number of women involved in paid employment increased from 3.3 million in 1914 to 4.9 million by 1918. Many had left domestic service for factory work and a whole range of other jobs. However, when the war ended, many women had to give up their jobs to men returning from the war. Women were 'rewarded' for their wartime contributions by the 1918 Representation of the People Act which gave women aged 30 or over the vote. Before the war, the suffragettes had waged a militant campaign for the right to vote but in 1914 they had suspended their campaigning for the war's duration. However, the 1918 legislation did not give women equality with men as men aged 21 and over were entitled to vote.

In terms of the political system, unlike in countries like Russia, Germany, and Italy, the war did not have a significant impact on Britain in that confidence in the democratic system was affirmed by the wartime experience and by victory.

3.1.3 Italy

The impact of the First World War on Italy (1915–18)

Three years of largely static, trench-warfare cost Italy 600,000 dead. In October 1917 Italy suffered a major defeat at Caporetto, which saw the Italians retreat over 100 km.

- The war worsened the political and social divisions within Italy, rather than uniting Italians as many of the politicians who had argued for Italy's intervention in the war had hoped. Italian politicians, including the **Liberals** who had dominated Italian politics since Italy's unification, had been very divided over whether Italy should intervene in the First World War crisis. These divisions proved permanent and were one reason why the Liberals were unable to maintain their hold on power after the war.

- Six million men served in Italy's armed forces and many of them, particularly the junior officers and **NCOs** who were drawn largely from the lower middle class, were politicised by the experience. They blamed the liberal politicians for mismanaging the war and hated the **Socialists** for failing to support the war; many ex-soldiers turned to Mussolini's **Fascist movement** after the war.

- Industrial output expanded rapidly, for example, Fiat's production of vehicles went up by 500% during the war, while its workforce grew from 4,000 to 40,000. Inevitably this led to huge economic dislocation when the war ended, and the economy reverted to a peacetime footing.

- Inflation and food shortages were serious problems: prices went up by 400% between 1914 and 1918. The government spent 148,000 million lira on the war: twice the total government expenditure in the entire period 1861–1914. To finance

---

🔑 **KEY TERMS**

Liberals: Dominant political groupings in Italy prior to 1918. Liberals sought to maintain an elected system of government and civil liberties. However, they tended to represent the interests of the propertied classes, rather than the working classes.

NCOs: An abbreviation for non-commissioned officers. Ranks in an army, such as corporal, which were between the officers, on the one hand, and the ordinary private soldiers on the other.

Socialists: Political groups who sought to reduce inequalities of wealth; in Italy, the largest Socialist party was the PSI. They were internationalist in outlook and had opposed Italy's entry into the First World War.

Fascist movement: Aggressively nationalistic and authoritarian political movement created by Mussolini.

the war, the Italian government borrowed hugely, predominantly from the USA and Britain.

- During the war, there was growing unrest among the industrial workers as they endured price inflation, food and commodity shortages and military-style discipline in the factories. In August 1917 the police and army killed 50 protestors in Turin after working-class demonstrations against prices and shortages. The increased militancy of the industrial workers was reflected in the expansion of trade union membership and the growth of the PSI (the Socialist Party).

The post-war crisis in Italy (1918–22)

Italy faced serious economic, social and political crises after the First World War, which the Liberals who had controlled Italy for the past 50 years proved incapable of coping with. These conditions provided Mussolini with the opportunity to create and then rapidly expand his new Fascist movement.

The advent of democracy and mass politics

During the war, the Liberals had promised the extension of the vote to all adult men and duly introduced universal male suffrage in December 1918 and **proportional representation** in August 1919. However, the Liberals did not adapt to the new era of mass politics. As the historian Martin Kitchen has observed, it was 'no longer possible to control parliament by the traditional liberal methods of political horse trading and influence peddling known as *trasformismo*' (Kitchen, 2014, p. 214). In the 1919 elections, the Liberals gained less than half the seats in the Chamber (elected house of parliament) while the PSI and the newly formed Catholic party, the PPI, or *Popolari*, emerged as the biggest parties.

Italian politics became increasingly fragmented

The three major political parties (Socialists, Liberals and Popolari) or groupings (the Liberals were not a united party as such) proved incapable of working together to form strong **coalition governments**. The result was a series of short-lived coalitions, which undermined many Italians' confidence in the democratic parliamentary system. In 1921 the rise of the Fascists as an electoral force and the breakaway by revolutionary socialists to found the Italian Communist Party (PCI) increased the political polarisation and instability. In all, there were 13 different groupings in the Chamber in 1921.

Nationalist anger at the 'mutilated victory'

The Italian Nationalists were furious at the terms of the peace treaties signed in Paris in 1919 and they were able to create the impression that the Italian Army had been betrayed by Italy's allies who failed to give Italy greater territorial gains and by the Liberal Italian government led by Vittorio Orlando for not standing up sufficiently for Italy's interests. In 1919 Italy was granted South Tyrol, Trieste, and Trentino (all from the former Austro-Hungarian Empire) but did not receive Fiume or Dalmatia (which instead were awarded to Yugoslavia).

The Italian nationalist poet, Gabriele D'Annunzio, coined the phrase 'the mutilated victory', to characterise the disappointment Italian patriots felt at having won the war but 'lost the peace'. D'Annunzio led a force of 2,000 ex-soldiers and occupied Fiume

---

KEY TERMS

Proportional representation: Voting system in elections whereby a party that wins a certain percentage of the votes cast gets the same percentage of the seats in parliament.

Trasformismo: Literally 'transformation'. This was the system whereby changes in government were engineered by the leaders

of the main parties reaching deals among themselves, rather than as a result of the votes cast by the electorate.

Coalition governments: Governments formed by two or more political parties sharing power and running the country together.

in September 1919 in protest at the Italian government's decision to hand it over to Yugoslavia as the Treaty of St Germain dictated. The occupation continued until the fovernment, led by the liberal Prime Minister Giolitti, ejected D'Annunzio and his paramilitaries in December 1920.

Economic crisis and social unrest

The transition from wartime to peacetime economy proved very painful for Italy. Prices increased by 50% in 1918–20, hitting those on fixed incomes and those with savings particularly hard. 2.5 million Italian soldiers were demobilised and many found no jobs to return home to. Unemployment peaked at two million in late 1919. In 1921 the US government placed strict restrictions on immigration into the USA; this worsened the plight of the poor in southern Italy: many of whom had, in the past, sought escape in the form of emigration to the USA.

The years 1919–20 were marked by huge social unrest and became known as the *Biennio Rosso*. Radical socialists hoped to copy Russia and stage a Bolshevik-style revolution, while many middle- and upper-class Italians feared for their property in the event of an Italian 'October' Revolution.

Once the war ended many southern peasants, led by socialist land leagues, seized uncultivated land left fallow by large landowners. The liberal governments of 1919–20 sanctioned these seizures by passing the Visochi and Falconi Decrees, giving the peasants legal title to the land they had taken, which shocked many of the landed classes. In the north, peasant unions forced landlords to cut rents and increase wages.

The trade unions grew enormously; the socialist CGL's membership increased from 250,000 in 1918 to over two million by 1920 and the Catholic unions' membership rose from 160,000 to 1,600,000 in the same period. With this growth came an increase in militancy. In 1919, and, again in 1920, more than one million workers went on strike, culminating in a four-week 'occupation of the factories' in August–September when, in many cities, industrial workers staged sit-ins and took over the factories, setting up factory committees.

Social unrest spawned growing political violence. Many ex-servicemen's experience of fighting meant that after the war they sought to resolve political and social issues by confrontation and physical force. From 1920 onwards, Fascist 'squads', recruited mainly from ex-servicemen, broke up strikes and closed down socialist and trade union offices throughout much of northern and central Italy. The Fascists also fought the socialists and trade union members in the countryside; from autumn 1920 through to the summer of 1921, they wrested control of large areas of rural northern and central Italy away from socialists, trade unions and peasant leagues.

The rise of Fascism

In the post-war years, Mussolini and the Fascists exploited middle- and upper-class fears of socialist revolution, which appeared to many during the *Biennio Rosso* to be imminent. For many property owners, the Fascist *squadristi* seemed to offer the best defence against a left-wing revolution and this was a key reason why the 1921 elections saw the PNF (Fascists) win 35 seats in the Italian Parliament.

Many Fascists were recruited from the middle class and, especially the lower middle class: small farmers, skilled craftsmen, shopkeepers, teachers and civil servants. This social group had dominated the ranks of the junior officers and NCOs during the war

KEY TERMS

Biennio Rosso: 'The Two Red Years'. A period marked by an upsurge of miltant action by left-wing groups.

and the war had politicised them. After the war, they resented the privileged position and power of the ruling classes but were also hostile to the trade unions and socialists, fearing that they would be levelled down to the status of the labouring classes.

The rise of Fascism is a remarkable phenomenon; from just a few hundred members in 1919, the movement grew to over 300,000 by October 1922. This support enabled Mussolini to put pressure on King Victor Emmanuel to appoint him prime minister after he organised the so-called 'March on Rome' by thousands of his black-shirted squads.

3.2 International Effects of the First World War

Because of the 'total' nature of the First World War, its impact on the combatant nations was far greater than that of previous conflicts. Similarly, that it involved so many countries and was fought across several fronts, spanning Western, Eastern and South Eastern Europe, parts of Africa and the Middle East (and to a much lesser extent Asia), meant that its effects were felt far more widely.

- The war's total direct cost is an estimated $180 billion (about $3,240 billion in today's values); its indirect cost $150 billion (about $2,700 billion in today's values).
- The economies of the combatant nations consequently suffered hugely as they battled to deal with the inevitable pains of readjusting from a wartime to peacetime economy, huge debts and high inflation (resulting from the increased supply of paper money issued by European governments during the war and shortages of goods caused by the war's dislocation of trade).

Several countries endured major economic crises in 1919-23, with Italy and Germany both suffering from high levels of unemployment and inflation. In Germany, the combined effects of rising prices and huge government borrowing during the war, reparations imposed by the Treaty of Versailles and reckless printing of paper money in the early 1920s, resulted in the devastating Hyper-Inflation Crisis of 1923.

3.2.1 Economic and Financial Consequences

KEY ISSUES

What changes did the war bring about in international trade and finance?

- At the start of the war, the USA was a debtor nation, borrowing more than it lent, but the war resulted in the USA becoming the world's leading creditor, providing massive loans to Britain and several of its other allies, notably France and Italy.

RECIPIENT COUNTRY	PRE-ARMISTICE (CASH)	POST ARMISTICE (CASH & SUPPLIES)	TOTAL DEBT
Britain	$3,696 million	$581 million	$4,277 million
France	$1,970 million	$1,434.8 million	$3,404.8 million
Italy	$1,031 million	$617 million	$1,648 million

- The USA continued to play the dominant role as international creditor in the 1920s, providing $7.6 billion in loans abroad.
- The USA's insistence on the full repayment of its wartime loans to Europe was shortsighted as it undermined the financial health of the USA's European trade partners, which probably contributed to the Great Depression of the 1930s. By the end of 1926, all of the major European debtor nations had signed repayment agreements with the USA.
- The First World War had a massive impact on the pattern of international trade as the USA exploited Britain, France, and Germany's concentration on production of war goods to expand its commercial penetration of Latin America. Similarly, Japan benefitted enormously in increasing its trade in Asia at the expense of Britain, Germany and France.

As William Keylor puts it:

> From an economic point of view, the First World War was won by the United States and Japan, both of which avoided territorial destruction or loss of life on a large scale while acquiring economic predominance within their respective geographic regions.

Keylor, 1984, p. 105

This shift in the economic balance of power is confirmed by the statistics for world trade in the period 1913–29.

Whereas the total value of world exports rose by two-thirds, there were major disparities between the growth of individual countries' exports:

- Britain's exports increased by just 15%.
- Germany's exports increased by 33%.
- France's exports increased by 50%.
- US exports increased by 100%.
- Japan's exports increased by 200%.

In the 1920s, US administrations followed a protectionist policy, imposing high import duties on foreign goods coming into the USA: for example, the Fordney–McCumber Tariff (1922), which damaged international trade. In the 1920s, the USA averaged a $1 billion trade surplus with Europe.

3.2.2 The Geopolitical Impact and Consequences for International Relations

---

KEY ISSUES

Did the First World lay the foundations for the Second World War?

The First World War did not prove to be, as President Wilson had predicted, 'the war to end all wars'. Within twenty years the Second World War broke out. After the Versailles Treaty was signed in 1919, the supreme commander of Allied forces, French General Ferdinand Foch, famously commented that, '[t]his is not a peace. This is an armistice for 20 years.' Foch was predicting that the Paris Peace settlement would not prevent Germany from seeking a war of revenge: that it would weaken Germany temporarily, but that Germany would recover its strength and go to war to regain its lost territories. Many Frenchmen at the time believed that Germany should have been treated more harshly, so it could not start another war. This is why, in 1919, France demanded that the Rhineland and Saarland should be made independent or handed over to France, neither of which happened; instead, the Rhineland was demilitarised and the Saarland taken from Germany for 15 years.

While one might reject the view that the First World War and the Versailles Treaty made another general European war inevitable, it is clear that both had far-reaching consequences for international relations and made the preservation of peace very difficult.

The Paris Peace settlement, which followed the end of the war, consisted of a series of individual treaties that dealt with the defeated powers.

Table 3.1: The individual treaties of the Paris Peace settlement

TREATY	DATE	DEALT WITH
Versailles	1919	Germany
Neuilly	1919	Bulgaria
St Germain	1919	Austria
Trianon	1920	Hungary
Sèvres	1920	Turkey
Lausanne	1923	Turkey

The collapse of four great empires and the creation of the successor states

The First World War and the peace settlement in 1919–20 shattered the old balance of power that had prevailed for so long between the Austro-Hungarian, German, and Russian Empires:

- The Russian Empire had collapsed in February 1917.
- The Hohenzollerns (in Germany) and Habsburgs (in Austria–Hungary) abdicated in November 1918.
- In South Eastern Europe, the Ottoman Empire (Turkish) lost its extensive lands in North Africa and the Middle East and soon became a republic under Mustapha Kemal Attaturk.

The Paris Peace Treaties created or, perhaps more accurately, recognised a series of new small states in Central and Eastern Europe:

- Czechoslovakia
- Austria
- Poland
- Hungary
- Latvia
- Lithuania
- Finland.

They also recognised, in South Eastern Europe, Yugoslavia.

These successor states proved unable to stand up to the aggression of Hitler and Stalin in the 1930s, following Germany's economic recovery and rearmament under the Nazis and the rise of the USSR as an industrial and military power as a result of Stalin's Five-Year Plans.

The creation of a strong nationalist movement in Germany

Many Germans were intent on destroying Versailles, including Hitler, although Hitler's foreign policy was largely shaped by his racial ideas, and only partly by the Treaty of Versailles. Versailles created a desire for revenge.

A young Mao Zedong in China, reflecting on the Treaty of Versailles, wrote in 1919:

> I guarantee that in ten or twenty years, you Frenchmen will yet again have a splitting headache. Mark my words!

Quoted in Short, 1999, p. 96

KEY ISSUES

Why did most Germans see the terms imposed on their country as harsh, unfair, and inconsistent?

- Germany lost about 13% of its European territory and all of its overseas colonies.
- Germans especially resented the loss of German speakers to Poland (in West Prussia and part of Upper Silesia) and the permanent ban on union with German-speaking Austria, arguing that this contradicted Woodrow Wilson's Fourteen Points (January 1918) which put forward the idea that the map of Europe should be redrawn on the principle of **national self-determination.**

↳

KEY TERMS

Successor states: Term given to the new countries that were created in 1919--20 out of the former Austro-Hungarian, German, Ottoman, and Russian empires.

National self-determination: The principle that each people should be able to choose the government under which it lives and that peoples of the same race should be able to unite within a single state.

KEY ISSUES *(continued)*

Why did most Germans see the terms imposed on their country as harsh, unfair, and inconsistent?

- Reparations were regarded as excessively harsh, higher than Germany could afford to pay, and many Germans rejected the charge of war guilt, which was used to justify the demand that Germany pay compensation to the Allies.
- Furthermore, German national pride was offended by the military restrictions imposed by the Versailles '**diktat**': the German Army, formerly the most powerful in Europe, was reduced to a mere 100,000 men.

The war and subsequent Versailles Treaty destabilised Germany economically and politically

Both British Prime Minister David Lloyd-George and economist John Maynard Keynes (1919) feared this would happen. Reparations were certainly a cause of the 1923 Hyper-Inflation Crisis, as the German government sought to pay off its financial liabilities by printing more paper money; and, from 1924, to enable Germany to pay reparations, the Dawes Plan provided Germany with large loans but this made its economic prosperity dangerously reliant on their continuation. In 1929, the Wall Street Crash hit Germany harder than most countries because its economy was much more fragile and because the USA stopped its massive loans to Germany. Without the Wall Street Crash and Great Depression, the rise of Hitler and his aggressive foreign policy would have been extremely unlikely.

KEY ISSUES

An alternative view on whether the First World War made a second inevitable

Yet none of the above means that a second war was inevitable:

- The issue of reparations could have been dealt with differently by the German government and so not damaged the economy so much – Germany could have raised taxes to pay for reparations rather than printing more money.
- During 1924–29 German Foreign Minister Gustav Stresemann's policy of 'fulfilment' – of cooperating with Britain and France over the Versailles Treaty's terms – got results and led to an improvement in European relations, particularly at Locarno in 1925.
- Finally, even after Germany was plunged into economic and political crisis by the Wall Street Crash, the Nazis almost didn't get into power; the economic crisis peaked in 1932 and Nazi support fell in the second election of 1932.

The creation of German minorities

The peace settlement left German-speaking minorities outside Germany: in Czechoslovakia, Poland, and Austria. Hitler skilfully exploited this fact in the 1930s to take over Austria and Czechoslovakia.

The peace treaties created many boundary disputes

Boundary disputes caused lasting tensions between European states, particularly the successor states, for example: Poland resented Teschen being awarded to Czechoslovakia

KEY TERMS

Diktat: German for 'dictated' peace. Germans resented that their country had not been given the opportunity to negotiate the terms of the Versailles Treaty; it was imposed on Germany by the victor powers.

and Hungarian-Czechoslovakian relations were soured by Hungary's anger that many Hungarians were living in Czechoslovakia.

Italian resentment at the peace settlement

As already indicated above, many Italians were angry at the so-called 'mutilated victory'. The belief of many Italian nationalists that Italy had not received what France and Britain had promised to Italy in the Treaty of London (1915) helped Mussolini to power in 1922 and he pursued an aggressive foreign policy: for example: the invasion of Abyssinia in 1935, which undermined the League of Nations and the prospects for lasting international peace.

The peace settlement led to the immediate outbreak of war between Turkey and Greece

The terms of the Treaty of Sèvres (1920), which saw Turkey lose all of its Middle Eastern and North African territories and considerable land in Europe/Central Asia to Greece, provoked a nationalist uprising in Turkey led by Mustafa Kemal, which led to the establishment of a republic, replacing rule by the Sultan.

Turkey went to war with Greece in 1920–23 in an attempt to win back territories taken from Turkey and awarded to Greece. The Allies demonstrated that they were not prepared to use force to defend the Paris settlement and instead, by the Treaty of Lausanne (1923), they recognised that Turkey had regained Smyrna, Eastern Thrace, part of Armenia and some of the Aegean islands. In addition, the Treaty of Sèvres' clauses relating to the imposition of international control of the Straits of the Dardanelles and the establishment of an international commission to oversee Turkey's finances were dropped. The Straits were, however, to remain a demilitarised zone.

Britain and France proved reluctant to defend the peace settlement made in 1919

This was partly because both countries were weakened financially by the war and both disarmed to a significant degree after 1919. In Britain's case, many politicians came to believe that the Treaty of Versailles had been too harsh on Germany and the policy of appeasement in the mid-late 1930s was in part a consequence of that conviction. Instead of standing up to Hitler, up until 1939, Britain made concessions to him: for example, the Anglo-German Naval Convention (1935) under which Britain agreed Germany could build up a navy 35% the size of Britain's.

France's reluctance to defend the peace settlement stemmed from a feeling of insecurity following the USA's refusal to approve the Anglo-American Guarantee (of military assistance) that Woodrow Wilson had promised in 1919 and, consequently, Britain's failure to abide by it. Furthermore, French politicians and generals were convinced that France, on its own, could not stand up to Germany: French military planning in the interwar period became wholly defensive, epitomised by the construction of the Maginot Line, a huge series of fortifications on the Franco-German border, from the late 1920s.

The creation of the League of Nations

Arguably the League of Nations, created by the peace settlement as a reaction to the horrors of the First World War and the consequent desire to avoid another war like it in the future, was flawed from the outset and therefore unlikely to be able to maintain international peace.

The French had wanted the League to take the form of a military alliance (along the lines of NATO), but instead it became a loose association of nations. The British succeeded in pushing for a more flexible association of all nations, not just a league of democracies as Wilson had originally envisaged.

For Woodrow Wilson, the establishment of the League had been a key priority. However, the USA never joined the League because the US Senate opposed American membership and refused to ratify the Versailles Treaty. This was a huge blow to the League since enforcement of its decisions without the financial and military resources of the USA would prove extremely difficult. Without American membership, France and Britain, the most powerful countries in the League, proved unwilling to act as world policemen and this was demonstrated by the failure to stand up to Japanese and Italian aggression (over Manchuria and Abyssinia respectively) in the 1930s.

The USA retreated into isolationism

As discussed above, the USA's withdrawal from international commitments after 1919 had major consequences for international relations. Not only did the USA undermine the League's prospects for success by failing to join it, but also Japanese and German aggression was successful in the 1930s partly because the USA refrained from intervening. Many American politicians and much of the US public were keen to avoid a repetition of the financial and human costs of the First World War.

ESSAY-WRITING ACTIVITIES

Below, you will find two essay questions, which cover most of the issues that I have dealt with in the revision guide. By examining these questions, you will be able to test your understanding and recall of the material and also practise your essay-writing skills. I have included, firstly, a student's answer to a question on the First World War and invite you to make your own evaluation of its strengths and weaknesses and to make suggestions about what you would do differently. I have included my own notes for you to compare your response to. For the second question, I have presented my own essay on the similarities and differences in the effects of the First World War on two countries, and left space for you to add your own points.

---

1. To what extent did any one 20th-century war break out as a result of miscalculation rather than premeditation on the part of the countries involved?

Below is an answer to a question on the causes of the First World War. Read it through and, as you do, consider what its strengths and weaknesses are and how you might improve it.

It is not intended to be a model answer. It would probably gain 5 IB points, in the region of 8/9 out of 15.

After the essay, you will find my own thoughts on the essay and suggestions for improving it, as well as some observations on what the characteristics of a good introduction and a good conclusion are.

One of the most complex historical debates about the origins of the First World War centres on the question of whether the governments of Germany and Austria-Hungary wanted war with Serbia, and whether they realised that such a war was likely to escalate into a general European conflict. Previous crises in the Balkans, such as the Austrian annexation of Bosnia-Herzegovina in 1908, and the First and Second Balkan Wars of 1912–13 had been managed by the Powers in a way that avoided inter-Power armed conflict. Why then did war break out in 1914, and why did it come to involve all five great powers?

There is little doubt that the Austrian government sought a war with Serbia rather than her diplomatic humiliation. The ultimatum sent on 23 July 1914, and the attitude of Conrad, chief of the Austrian general staff, are firm evidence of that. That the Austrians asked Berlin for a 'blank cheque', which was granted on 5 July, is proof that they saw the danger of Russian involvement in the conflict. For the Germans' part, the Riezler diaries and the actions and words of Chancellor Bethman-Hollweg and Wilhelm II make it clear that the 'blank cheque' was granted in the awareness that the Russians would intervene militarily. The Germans prodded Austria-Hungary into action, though they knew that their own war plans would commit them to a war against France as well as Russia. The only element in the escalation which Bethmann-Hollweg and the Kaiser failed to foresee was the involvement of the British. Their panic on 28–29 July when they realised that the British were likely to intervene is evidence of this. By then the pressure on civilian politicians in both Germany and Russia to mobilise at the earliest moment was intense, and the military logic of the situation was pursued by both countries. The only thing that, from the point of view of the Central Powers, got out of control in 1914 was Great Britain.

An adequate appraisal of the First World War's origins demands a long-term consideration of international relations. German unification created the potential for conflict in Europe because it disrupted the balance of power and left the French eager for revenge. The Turkish Empire's long-term decline and the rise of Balkan nationalism had been creating problems for the Austrians and expansionist opportunities for the Russians throughout the 19th century. In spite of Bismarck's Dreikaiserbund, successive Balkan crises in the 1870s and 1880s drove Russian and Austria-Hungary further apart. In signing the 1879

Dual Alliance with Austria Bismarck bowed to a racial geopolitical logic which dictated that Germany must side with Austria in any conflict with Russia. In trying to maintain, by means of the Reinsurance Treaty of 1887, some diplomatic link with Russia Bismarck was merely papering over a widening crack. Yet even before Bismarck's resignation in 1890 and despite his pacific foreign policy, Russia and France had begun to draw together. Their 1894 alliance was not merely the result of Wilhelmine foreign policy; the very existence of a united Germany created a mutual interest between them.

The colonialism, *Weltpolitik* and naval expansion favoured by Wilhelm II served to bring together Britain and France in the Entente Cordiale of 1904, and to draw Britain so far out of her traditional isolation as to sign pacts with Japan (1902) and Russia (1907). The 'encirclement' which so troubled German strategists in the decade up to 1914 was thus largely the product of German foreign policy since 1890, and incidents such as the First and Second Moroccan Crises (1906, 1911) helped to preserve the anti-German rapprochement between Britain and France. The war plans drawn up by the powers after 1900 reflected these realities, and the Schlieffen Plan was based on the self-fulfilling assumption that Germany would have to tackle France and Russia simultaneously.

Internal political factors also disposed the powers to war in the period 1900-14. The failure of the Kaiser's *sammlungspolitik*, the rise of the SPD and the political row over the Zabern incident helped persuade the Kaiser that a successful war would offer an escape from the dilemmas posed by the Bismarckian constitution. For Austria-Hungary, the whole point of the conflict with Serbia was to deal a fatal blow to that South Slav nationalism which threatened to tear the Empire apart. In all the belligerent countries there was a fashionable political Darwinism in the air, which fostered the belief that war was an engine of political and national progress. The occasion of war in the summer of 1914 – an Archduke's chauffeur taking a wrong turning – may have been accidental, but the European situation made a general war a high probability.

Your thoughts on the essay's strengths:

_____

_____

_____

_____

_____

Your thoughts on the essay's weaknesses:

_____

_____

_____

_____

_____

_____

_____

What additional/different points you would include if you were answering this question:

_____

_____

_____

_____

_____

_____

_____

An evaluation of Essay 1

The essay has certain *strengths*:

- ⊘ It is very well informed in terms of subject knowledge.
- ⊘ It demonstrates an understanding of the main causes of the war.
- ⊘ The communication is very clear

However, the essay has several major *weaknesses*:

- ⊗ The introduction does not indicate the line of argument/thesis that the essay will develop, which a good introduction should do, and, the second half of the introduction does not address the question.

- ⊗ There is no proper conclusion; the conclusion is really just the last sentence. New points should not be introduced into the conclusion; instead clearly and consistently restate your main arguments.

- ⊗ There is no historiography or awareness of differing perspectives. Given that this question is one of the most contentious of all time, an examiner would certainly expect a high-level answer to show some awareness of the differing historical interpretations relevant to this question. In this case, some reference to how A. J. P. Taylor viewed the war as an accidental one, whereas Fischer saw it as a war deliberately engineered by Germany, would be helpful. You do not need to pack historiography into your answers but showing an awareness of relevant historical interpretations or some other evidence of differing perspectives is required to gain a mark in the top 2-mark bands.

- ⊗ The focus of the essay drifts away from the wording of the question in several places. For example, paragraphs three and four identify what some of the long-term factors causing the war were but do not explain how these factors actually caused the war. The candidate does not link these paragraphs to the question.

One of the main ways of ensuring that your answer is tightly linked to the question is to make sure that the first sentence of each paragraph contains a thesis statement/point of analysis that directly and clearly addresses the question and that reflects what you say in the rest of the paragraph.

2. Compare and contrast the effects of one 20th-century war on two countries involved in it.

Below this paragraph, you will see an essay that I have written relating to similarities and differences in the effects of the First World War on Germany and Russia. After my answer, I have left space so you can add more points of your own and examples to illustrate the key points. Finally, there is space for you to write your own conclusion.

In answering this question with regards to the First World War, the two countries selected will be Germany and Russia. Both countries suffered from huge economic problems during and after the war resulting from the unprecedented scale of the armies involved and of the munitions required in the first general European war fought since the advent of full-blown industrialisation. Furthermore, both countries were destabilised politically by the First World War and, in both cases, the ruling systems of government collapsed. However, the effects on Russia were more far-reaching because the war accentuated huge pre-existing social, economic and political tensions and Russia's relative backwardness made it less resilient to the stresses of the war compared to the more industrially, socially and politically developed Germany. In Russia's case, Lenin's observation that 'war is the midwife of revolution' proved correct and Russia endured two revolutions, whereas Germany, although apparently facing revolutionary pressures in 1918, avoided revolution.

Both Russia and Germany mobilised their economies and populations fully in what is regarded as the first example of 'total' warfare; consequently, the socio-economic impact was unprecedented. Inflation and food shortages affected both countries, with Germany increasing the amount of paper money in circulation by 1,141% but Russia was less able to cope than the much more developed industrial economy of Germany and the scale of Russian inflation far outstripped Germany's during the war, with prices, by February 1917, 400% higher than in August 1914.

In both countries, the economic problems caused by the First World War did not end in 1918. In Russia, inflation continued to soar, resulting in the collapse of the rouble in 1918, and, by 1921, industrial production was only 20% what it had been in 1913, although this was the result of the combined effect of both the First World War and the Russian Civil War (1918–21). In Germany's case, the combined impact of huge government borrowing during the war, the loss of economic resources due to the impact of the Treaty of Versailles imposed on Germany when it lost the war, and the reparations burden imposed by Versailles, led to the hyper-inflation crisis of 1923.

In political terms, the effect of the First World War on both countries, was to destabilise them and bring about the end of their imperial systems, represented by the Romanovs and Hohenzollerns. Both Nicholas II and Wilhelm II were discredited by their countries' performance in the war, although this did not become clear in Germany's case until 1918 as up until then most Germans appear to have remained confident that Germany would win the war. In Russia's case, the February Revolution of 1917, was the product of the economic and political stresses imposed by the war, compounded by Nicholas II's decision to make himself commander-in-chief in 1915, meaning that subsequent Russian defeats were blamed on the tsar personally. However, it can be argued that, with Russia, the war merely accelerated the inevitable decline of tsarism as many historians see Nicholas II's failure to adapt the Russian monarchy prior to 1914 as fatal for tsarism because it left the monarchy increasingly isolated, as evidenced by the disillusionment of the Octobrists at Nicholas' failure to work with the Duma. In Russia, the decision of the new Provisional Government to carry on in the war, led to mounting defeats, particularly the so-called Kerensky Offensive, and economic problems, with inflation rising a further 600% in 1917, culminating in the Bolsheviks seizing power in the October Revolution. The Bolsheviks subsequently radically transformed Russia socially and economically, destroying the old ruling elites in the process. In Germany, by early 1918, impending military defeat, growing economic crisis and increasing political unrest, seemed to threaten a revolution but, unlike in Russia, this did not happen because the Kaiser abdicated in November 1918 and a new democratic government came to power. Unlike the Russian Provisional Government, the new Weimar Republic in Germany was able to survive because it immediately signed the armistice of November 1918 whereas the Provisional Government had fatally decided to continue Russia's participation in the war when it came to power in March 1917.

The long-term political effects of the war were very different because in Russia's case the war led to the establishment of a left-wing dictatorship that remained in power for another seven decades, whereas in Germany's case, the war led to the creation of a democratic republic that survived until 1933 when it was overthrown by Hitler. Also, although both countries were destabilised politically for a considerable period of time following the end of the war, the destabilisation was much more extreme in Russia, with full-scale civil war erupting in 1918, following Russia's withdrawal from the war in March 1918. In Germany, the Weimar Republic was faced by a number of left- and right-wing attempts to overthrow it in the period 1919–23, such as the Spartacist Rising (1919) and the Kapp Putsch (1920), with those on the left seeking to emulate the Bolshevik revolution and those Nationalists, on the right, rejecting the 'November criminals' of the new democratic government for 'stabbing in the back' the German Army by surrendering in November 1918 and then signing the shameful Treaty of Versailles in 1919. However, the scale of upheaval in Germany in this period nowhere near matched that of the Russian Civil War. Nonetheless, some historians argue that Weimar's birth out of the military defeat and humiliation of 1918–19 made it very unlikely that the democratic system would survive. Nonetheless, the relative stability of the Stresemann era of 1924–28 would indicate that the First World War and the subsequent Treaty of Versailles did not doom democracy to fail in Germany.

Both countries had harsh peace terms imposed on them when they dropped out of the war and both were to be isolated diplomatically. Russia lost approximately 20% of its territory, including Latvia, Lithuania, Estonia and Finland, as a result of the Treaty of Brest-Litovsk of March 1918, although the Bolsheviks did regain the Ukraine and Georgia by 1921, which were incorporated into the new USSR. German losses at Versailles were substantial too but not as great as Russia's, with 13% of Germany's territory, including Alsace-Lorraine and half of Upper Silesia, being taken away. Both countries were denied admission to the newly created League of Nations in 1920 and were regarded with suspicion by the international community. However, in Germany's case this proved more short-lived as, following the Locarno Conference of 1925, it was invited into the League of Nations. The USSR continued to be largely ostracised by the most of the world right through into the 1930s.

Russia and Germany both suffered huge economic and political destabilisation as a result of the First World War. In Russia, mounting economic problems and military defeats led to the Romanov dynasty being swept away, and, following a second revolution in October 1917, the first communist regime in history came into power, which radically transformed Russian socially, politically and economically and which led it to being ostracised by most of the international community for the next 20 years. Although, the more advanced Germany coped better in handling the economic and military challenges of the war, impending military defeat led to the collapse of the Hohenzollern dynasty in November 1918. Yet, in Germany's case the political transformation resulting from the war was less radical and, consequently, the traditional ruling elites maintained their privileged positions and, internationally, although Germany was temporarily isolated at the end of the war, by 1925, it had largely been rehabilitated.

Your points/examples of similarity:

_____

_____

_____

_____

_____

Your points/examples of difference:

_____

_____

_____

_____

_____

_____

_____

_____

Your conclusion:

_____

_____

_____

_____

_____

_____

_____

GLOSSARY

A

ALSACE-LORRAINE Rich industrial region taken from France.

ATTRITION The strategy of wearing down an enemy by a series of offensives, causing the enemy to reach the point at which their resources and will to go on expired before their own did.

B

BALKANS Area in South-Eastern Europe, so-called because of the mountain range running through it.

BIENNIO ROSSO 'The Two Red Years'. A period marked by an upsurge of miltant action by left-wing groups.

BOER WAR War between Great Britain and the Boer republics in South Africa (1899–1902).

BOLSHEVIK Political group committed to abolishing private property who seized power in Russia in 1917.

C

CENTRAL POWERS Term used to refer to Germany, Austria-Hungary and their allies.

COALITION GOVERNMENTS Governments formed by two or more political parties sharing power and running the country together.

COMMUNISTS Political groups aiming to abolish private property as the result of a revolution. In Germany, the Communists sought to copy the success of Lenin's Bolsheviks who seized control in Russia in 1917.

CONSCIENTIOUS OBJECTORS People who refuse to do military service because they oppose war and fighting on moral or religious grounds.

CONSCRIPTION Compulsory military service.

CROSSING THE T Naval tactic in which a line of warships crosses in front of a line of enemy ships, so that they can open fire with all their guns, while the enemy ships can only use their forward guns.

D

DEPTH CHARGE An anti-submarine weapon which consisted of a canister filled with explosives that was dropped off the stern of a ship. It would explode at a predetermined depth.

DIKTAT German for 'dictated' peace. Germans resented that their country had not been given the opportunity to negotiate the terms of the Versailles Treaty; it was imposed on Germany by the victor powers.

DUMA The Russian Parliament.

E

ENTENTE CORDIALE French for 'friendly agreement'. Term by which the Anglo-French treaty was known. It was not a military alliance but a diplomatic understanding.

ENTENTE POWERS Term used to refer to Britain, France, Russia and their allies. Often the Entente Powers were referred to as 'the Allies' or 'Allied Powers'.

THE EASTERN FRONT The area of Eastern Europe, chiefly on Russia's western borders, where much of the fighting in the First World War took place between Russia, Germany, and Austria-Hungary.

F

FASCIST MOVEMENT Aggressively nationalistic and authoritarian political movement created by Mussolini.

G

GNP An abbreviation for Gross National Product. The total value of goods and services produced by a country.

GREAT DEPRESSION The disastrous economic downturn that affected the USA and most industrialised economies in the early to mid-1930s, triggered by the Wall Street Crash.

H

HABSBURG The ruling family of the Austro-Hungarian Empire.

I

IMPERIALISM Policy whereby a country seeks to expand its territory to create an empire outside its existing borders. In the nineteenth and early twentieth centuries, several European powers competed in acquiring larger and larger overseas empires.

K

KAISER German term for 'Emperor'. Wilhelm II was Kaiser from 1888 to 1918.

L

LIBERALS Dominant political groupings in Italy prior to 1918. Liberals sought to maintain an elected system of government and civil liberties. However, they tended to represent the interests of the propertied classes, rather than the working classes.

N

NATIONAL SELF-DETERMINATION The principle that each people should be able to choose the government under which it lives and that peoples of the same race should be able to unite within a single state.

NATIONALISM   Pride and belief in promoting the strength of one's own country, putting its interests first, even if at the expense of other countries.

NATIONALISTS   Political groups who seek to make their country as strong as possible and who prioritise putting their countries' interests ahead of those of other countries. In the case of German nationalists, they also stood for the union of all German-speakers within a single German state.

NCOs   An abbreviation for non-commissioned officers. Ranks in an army, such as corporal, which were between the officers, on the one hand, and the ordinary private soldiers on the other.

P

PAN-SLAVISM   Belief in the solidarity and unity of the Slavic peoples across Eastern Europe; Pan-Slavs in Russia believed that Russia had the duty to protect their fellow Slavs living within the Ottoman and Austro-Hungarian Empires.

PLAN VII   France's pre-1914 war plan for a French offensive across the German border to retake Alsace-Lorraine in the event of a war with Germany.

PROPORTIONAL REPRESENTATION   Voting system in elections whereby a party that wins a certain percentage of the votes cast gets the same percentage of the seats in parliament.

R

REICHSTAG   Elected lower house of the German Parliament.

REPARATIONS   Germany was obliged by the Treaty of Versailles to pay £6,600 million in financial compensation to France, Britain, Italy and Belgium for damages inflicted during the First World War.

S

SALIENT   A piece of territory held by one side in a conflict that juts out into enemy territory and is surrounded by it on a number of sides.

SLAVS   Racial group in South Eastern and Eastern Europe that includes the Serbs and Russians.

SOCIALISTS   Politicians committed to ending inequalities in wealth and transferring power from the Kaiser to the Reichstag.

SOCIAL DARWINISM   The application of Charles Darwin's theory of the 'survival of the fittest' to the human species. In the nineteenth century there was a widespread belief that nations had to either survive through expansion or risk declining and being taken over by stronger nations.

SPLENDID ISOLATION   Term that was used to describe the Conservative Party's policy in the second half of the nineteenth century of keeping Britain out of any entangling alliances. The phrase is attributed to the Canadian politician, George Foster.

STRATEGIC BOMBING	The strategy of wearing down an enemy by sustained bombing raids, causing the enemy to reach the point at which their resources and will to go on expires. Strategic bombing targets industrial and civilian centres.
SUCCESSOR STATES	Term given to the new countries that were created in 1919–20 out of the former Austro-Hungarian, German, Ottoman, and Russian empires.

T

TACTICAL BOMBING	The use of aircraft to support ground troops by attacking enemy personnel, using machine guns and bombs.
TRASFORMISMO	Literally 'transformation'. This was the system whereby changes in government were engineered by the leaders of the main parties reaching deals among themselves, rather than as a result of the votes cast by the electorate.

W

WAR BONDS	Government debt certificates, guaranteeing repayment with interest by the government at the end of the war.
WEIMAR REPUBLIC	Germany between 1918 and 1933 is known as the Weimar Republic because it was in the town of Weimar that the constitution for the republic that was established in 1918, after the Kaiser abdicated, was drawn up.
WELTPOLITIK	The 'world' policy pursued by Wilhelm II from 1897 onwards, aimed at expanding Germany's overseas empire.
THE WESTERN FRONT	The area of north-western Europe, chiefly, Northern France and Belgium, where much of the fighting in the First World War took place.

BIBLIOGRAPHY

Best, A., Hanhimäki, J. M., Maiolo, J. A., and Schulze, K. E. 2004. *International History of the Twentieth Century*. London: Routledge

Bond, B. 1984. *War and Society in Europe, 1870–1970*. Bungay: Fontana

Churchill, W. 1931. *The World Crisis 1911–1918*. London: Thornton Butterworth

De Groot, G. 2001. *The First World War*. Basingstoke: Palgrave Macmillan

Ferguson, N. 2006. *The War of the World: Twentieth-Century Conflict and the Descent of the West*. New York: Penguin Press

Gilbert, M. 1969. *The European Powers, 1900–45*. London: Weidenfeld & Nicolson

Henig, R. 1993. *The Origins of the First World War*. 2nd edn. Abingdon: Routledge

Hobsbawm, E. 1994. *Age of Extremes: The Short Twentieth Century, 1914–1991*. London: Michael Joseph

Howard, M. 1970. *Studies in War and Peace*. Aldershot: Temple Smith

Hunt J., and Watson, S. 1990. *Britain and the Two World Wars*. Cambridge: Cambridge University Press

Joll, J., and Martel, G. 2007. *The Origins of the First World War*. 3rd edn. Abingdon: Routledge

Keegan, J. 1998. *The First World War*. London: Hutchinson

Kennedy, P. *The Rise and Fall of the Great Powers*. London: Unwin Hyman

Keylor, W. 1984. *The Twentieth Century World and Beyond: An International History*. Oxford: Oxford University Press

Keynes, J. M. 1919. *The Economic Consequences of the Peace*. New York: Harcourt, Brace and Howe

Kitchen, M. 2014. *Europe between the Wars*. 2nd edn. Abingdon: Routledge

Lamb, M., and Tarling, N. 2001. *From Versailles to Pearl Harbor: The Origins of the Second World War in Europe and Asia*. Basingstoke: Palgrave Macmillan

Messenger, C. 1995. *The Century of Warfare: Worldwide Conflict from 1900 to the Present Day*. London: Harper Collins

Morgan, K. O. ed. 1989. *The Oxford Mini History of Britain, Vol. V: The Modern Age*. Oxford: Oxford University Press

Pollard, S. ed. 1990. *Wealth & Poverty: An Economic History of the Twentieth Century*. Oxford: Oxford University Press

Ropp, T. 1959. *War in the Modern World*. Durham: Duke University Press,

Short, P. 1999. *Mao: A Life*. London: Hodder & Stoughton

Stewart, N. 2001. *The Changing Nature of Warfare, 1700–1945*. London: Hodder Education

Stone, N. 1975. *The Eastern Front: 1914–1917*. London: Hodder & Stoughton

Taylor, A. J. P. 1954. *The Struggle for Mastery in Europe.* Oxford: Oxford University Press

Taylor, A. J. P. 1969. *War by Time-table.* London: Macdonald

Terraine, J. *The Mighty Continent: A View of Europe in the Twentieth Century.* London: Futura Publications Limited

Western, J. R. 1965. *The End of European Primacy.* London: Blandford Press

Wolfson R., and Laver J. 1996. *Years of Change: European History, 1890–1945.* 2nd edn. London: Hodder & Stoughton

We hope this book has helped you with your studies especially as you prepare for exams.

Joe Gauci is also a History teacher on OSC's courses. You can read more about our Revision and Summer programmes on the following pages, as well as other resources we provide to help you achieve your best in the Diploma Programme.

MID IB SUMMER PROGRAMMES

Expert teaching consolidates year one learning and boosts confidence for year two, while social and cultural experiences offer personal enrichment and the chance to build friendships with students from around the world.

Approaches to Teaching

The summer provides a unique opportunity to review a full year of material in a short period of time. This allows our expert teachers to link together parts of the syllabus that are often taught months apart during the academic year. By weaving together concepts and theories, students are able to see how the different elements of each subject fits together and develop a more comprehensive understanding.

Students complete subject questionnaires prior to arrival so we can identify their individual needs. Our specialist IB teachers then craft their class content to meet those needs.

Students reinforce their IB skills and subject understanding, which will result in better grades. All advice given is accurate and effective because every OSC teacher is up-to-date with teacher training, syllabus changes, and the approach to examining their subject.

At the end of each course, teachers prepare personalised reports which provide recommendations for continued improvement.

CAMBRIDGE, UK

Cambridge is a world-renowned centre of innovation and academia. At the heart of the city is the University of Cambridge with its 31 colleges catering to a diverse and dynamic student population.

OSC students live and learn in Emmanuel College. Founded in 1584, the college has extensive grounds and offers an inspiring and peaceful atmosphere.

Outside of class, a full activity programme provides ample opportunity to explore the city as well as take part in quintessentially Cambridge activities such as punting along the River Cam. During the weekends, students participate in excursions to nearby attractions including trips to London and the Harry Potter Studios.

Cambridge is easily accessible from Stansted Airport, and coach services are available from other London-based airports including Heathrow.

BOSTON, USA

Students have the unique opportunity to explore two of the world's top five universities in one summer.

They reside at Harvard University based in Cambridge, MA, just across the Charles River from Boston. Very much a cool college town, there is plenty to safely explore within easy walking distance of our residence.

Each morning the students are transported, in an iconic yellow bus, to the Massachusetts Institute of Technology (MIT) for their lessons.

On top of the daily sports and social programme there are some wonderful day trip opportunities that include: whale watching, the Blue Man Group show, and a shopping trip to a popular outlet centre.

The Harvard residence halls are located a 30-minute drive from Logan International Airport where students usually jump into a waiting taxi.

ALL OSC SUMMERS INCLUDE:

› Teaching from experienced, trained, specialist, IB teachers

› Small teaching groups (maximum of 10 in subject-specific classes)

› Written reports for parents

› On-site experienced IB Director

› Daily cultural excursions, sports, and social activities

› Experience of life at a world-renowned university

› Supervised accommodation with a 24-hour Welfare and Social Activity Team

› A focus on building students' confidence and encouraging personal development

› One-to-one subject advice and careers guidance is available

Student Life

A summer spent with OSC will be full of fun, inspiring experiences, adventures in worldwide centres of culture and academia, and friendships formed with students from all over the world.

Our students love experiencing campus life and exploring their summer city through a range of activities, including: attending cultural attractions, playing sports, and visiting amusement parks.

Our Welfare and Social Activity Team are available 24 hours a day to handle any issues that arise and to help every individual get the most out of their summer.

There's also a unique opportunity for students to explore how the IB can support their future goals by attending the OSC University Fair.

'Everything was excellent! I've got new experiences, new friends and new knowledge.'

OSC STUDENT, 2017

'I have learned a huge amount in the past two weeks and feel extremely confident going into next year.'

OSC STUDENT, 2017

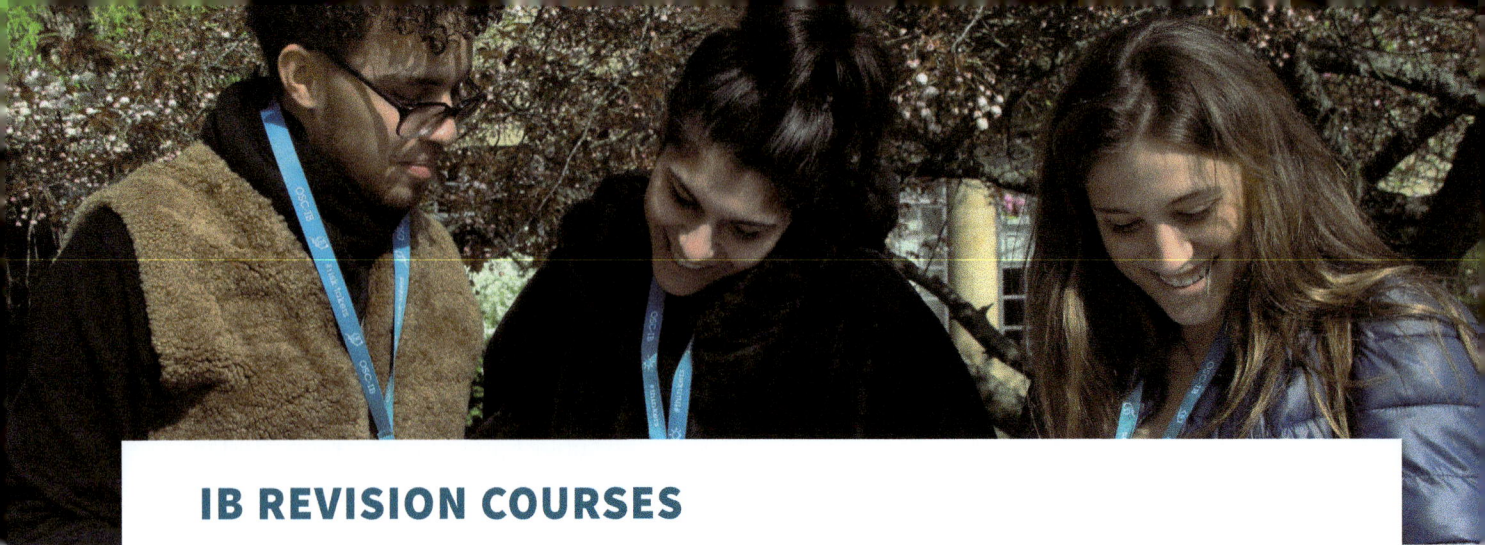

IB REVISION COURSES

A great revision course makes a student's life easier at a very stressful time and greatly improves their chances of getting into the university of their choice.

FEATURES OF A GREAT REVISION COURSE

The best IB teachers in schools will tell you that a short, intense revision course, with another great IB teacher, is invaluable. A fresh voice, with new ways of explaining the material, taking students through the key elements that they find challenging, can bring a new clarity and confidence in subjects at just the right time to support final grades. Different classmates and a new environment generate energy and motivation.

Experienced IB Teachers

You need an experienced IB teacher who is up-to-date with teaching and examining their subject. They will be familiar with the latest syllabus changes, the types of exam questions the IB are currently asking, and the latest expectations of the examiners. And you need someone who has taught students across a range of abilities, and understands what they find challenging.

Meeting Individual Needs

You need a carefully crafted programme for each student. The daily timetable must support intensive study. Class content should be based on student questionnaires, and then adapted as questions arise during the class. There is a huge benefit when students are streamed by grade. And as student needs are so diverse, even the best teachers should be supported by an experienced IB Director.

IB Revision Specialists

You need an IB teacher who has become a revision specialist, having developed effective and flexible approaches and materials over years of revision experience. They can confidently lead a group of students from different schools with different challenges and grade expectations to improve their outcomes.

'I really feel the urge to congratulate the teachers on their work of these 5 days. My son left home stressed, with no self-confidence, doubting if at all he would be able to pass the exams. He came back full of enthusiasm, motivated, full of praise of his teachers, suddenly full of energy. What did you do to him?! Since then he is working day and night and I am sure he will pass well! Thank you!'

OSC PARENT, 2017

OSC OXFORD - OSC'S PREMIUM REVISION COURSE

❯ Subjects streamed by grade

❯ 23 subjects available

❯ Attend for up to 6 subjects

❯ History classes streamed by options

❯ Overseen by an experienced IB Director

❯ Supervised accommodation with welfare team in case of illness or stress

Our Oxford course gives students a unique opportunity to live and work in the beautiful and inspiring Oxford University colleges.

Streaming classes by grade means that high flyers can focus on squeezing the last possible marks out of their exam answers, while those who are struggling more can be supported to find the most achievable marks in each exam question.

Being immersed in a calm but focused atmosphere with hundreds of other IB students in the same situation brings out the best in every individual.

OSC REVISION CENTRES

While it is impossible to match all the features of the huge Oxford course in smaller events, our amazing teaching team also delivers highly effective revision courses in the locations below. We can help you find local accommodation if necessary.

LONDON | BRUSSELS | MUNICH

DUBAI | SYDNEY | MELBOURNE | ADELAIDE

YOUR SCHOOL?

ALL REVISION COURSES FEATURE:

❯ 14 or 17.5 hours of teaching per subject

❯ Small classes of up to 10 students

❯ Separate HL & SL classes

❯ Total immersion in one subject at a time

❯ 2 hours of set and reviewed homework per evening

❯ Pre-course questionnaire that identifies students' needs

❯ Class notes available via online resource centre

❯ Students are never put with a teacher from their own school

OTHER OSC RESOURCES

OSC IB BLOGS

Thousands of free blog posts for students and teachers
- Written by experienced IB educators
- Searchable by subject

History-specific posts offer:
- Commentary on historical anniversaries
- Revision tips for students
- Syllabus and schedule notes for teachers
- Announcements on new OSC titles

OSC STUDENT TOOLS

On our website, students will find useful planning resources for download and use:
- A weekly revision planner
- A personal exam timetable

Newly released revised edition of *167 IB Secrets* by Tim Williams

This authoritative, practical, and frequently irreverent guide shows students how to navigate the complex pathways of the IBDP and gain extra points along the way.

167 IB SECRETS
Tim Williams
9781910689394

RECEIVE UPDATES

We are continually updating our materials and releasing new books.

Sign up at osc-ib.com/updates to keep up-to-date with the latest OSC information for History and other subjects you are interested in, and follow us on social media.

OXFORDSTUDYCOURSES   OSC_IB   OXFORDSTUDYCOURSES

FEEDBACK

We work with our authors to bring you the best IBDP resources to help you succeed in your studies, and welcome your feedback on this revision guide or any of OSC's resources.

Whether you have a suggestion, a correction or a review of the book, get in touch by email to **osc@osc-ib.com.**